No-Guilt Desserts

SWEET TEMPTATIONS   2

The skinny on choosing delicious low-calorie desserts.

LIGHT & LUSCIOUS CAKES   4

Here are all kinds of luscious ways to satisfy your cake cravings.

PLEASING PIES   20

Enjoy a guilt-free slice of your favorite pie—whether it's apple, cherry or lemon meringue.

BREAD BASKET TREATS   30

Indulge yourself with these wonderfully light home-baked breads, muffins and coffeecakes.

COOKIE MAGIC   40

Fill your cookie jar with scrumptious low-calorie goodies—perfect for anytime snacking.

COOL DELIGHTS   54

A marvelous medley of mousses, puddings, ice creams and other chilled treats.

FRUITFUL PLEASURES   72

Delectable fruit is featured in enticing crisps, cobblers, crepes and more.

EXCITING EXTRAS   84

Drinks, toppings, sauces and spreads to satisfy your sweet tooth but still keep you trim.

ACKNOWLEDGMENTS   91

INDEX   92

Sweet

◇◇◇

TEMPTATIONS

You Can Have Your Cake and Eat It, Too!

Like many people today, you're probably concerned about the way you eat. You'd like to make better choices about the foods you prepare, to cut down on calories, fat, cholesterol and sodium, but you also love to eat—especially dessert. Now there's a collection of recipes that will let you indulge in dessert *without* indulging in all the calories. With over 130 recipes from America's top food companies, NO-GUILT DESSERTS offers you a wide variety of dessert choices—from sinlessly rich cakes and cheesecakes, scrumptious cookies, sure-fire snacks, light ice creams and frozen yogurts, luscious pies, enticing breads, muffins and coffeecakes, fabulous fruit desserts and much, much more—all of them lower in calories and fat than you would expect.

Making Smart Choices

The American Heart Association offers guidelines to help people adjust their diets to try to prevent heart and vascular diseases and we've followed those guidelines in choosing recipes for this publication. The recipes that follow can help you make smart, healthy decisions about the desserts you prepare. Every recipe in this publication is followed by a nutritional chart that tells you the number of calories, the grams (g) of fat, the milligrams (mg) of sodium and the milligrams of cholesterol for each serving of that recipe. To be considered for this publication, recipes had to contain 300 calories or less per serving, and contain no more than 10 g of fat per serving. As an extra bonus, most of the desserts offered here are less than 200 calories per serving and many are even under 100 calories per serving.

Many of the recipes are low-sodium and low-cholesterol as well. These recipes contain less than 300 mg of sodium and less than 50 mg of cholesterol per serving. As you browse through the publication, you'll see that most of the recipes fall well below these numbers. You can easily find these recipes by looking for the color bars below each recipe title:

| **Under 200 Calories** |

| **Under 100 Calories** |

| **Low Sodium** |

| **Low *or* No Cholesterol** |

And, many recipes fall under more than one category.

The values of 300 calories, 10 g of fat, 300 mg sodium and 50 mg cholesterol per serving were chosen after careful consideration of a number of factors. The Food and Nutrition Board of the National Academy of Sciences proposes the Recommended Dietary Allowances (RDAs) for all nutritive components including calories, carbohydrates, fat, protein, amino acids, vitamins and minerals. The RDAs were most recently revised in 1989. The RDA for calories is broken down according to age groups and sex. For men between the ages of 19 and 50, for example, the RDA for total calorie intake is 2,900 calories per day. For women between the ages of 19 and 50 (who are neither pregnant nor lactating), it is 2,200 calories per day. Thus, the 300 calories or less per serving for the recipes in this publication represents only about 10 percent of the RDA for most men and about 14 percent of the RDA for most women.

The American Heart Association has recommended that total fat intake should contribute to less than 30 percent of one's calorie intake. For most women that amounts to about 660 calories from fat (or about 73 g of fat) per day; for most men about 870 calories or about 97 g of fat per day. Thus the 10 g of fat or less per serving for each recipe in this publication represents a reasonable amount for a single dessert in a single meal. The American Heart Association also recommends that sodium intake not exceed 3,000 mg a day, and cholesterol intake be less than 300 mg a day. The numbers we chose for recipes to be considered low-sodium (300 mg or less) or low-cholesterol (50 mg or less) are also well within these guidelines.

About the Nutritional Information

The analysis of each recipe includes all the ingredients that are listed in that recipe, except ingredients labeled as "optional" or "for garnish." If a range is given in the yield of a recipe ("Makes 6 to 8 servings," for example), the *higher* yield was used to calculate the per serving information. If a range is offered for an ingredient ("¼ to ⅛ teaspoon," for example), the *first* amount given was used to calculate the nutrition information. If an ingredient is presented with an option ("¼ cup margarine or butter," for example), the *first* item listed was used to calculate the nutrition information. Foods shown in photographs on the same serving plate or offered as "serve with" suggestions at the end of a recipe are *not* included in the recipe analysis unless stated in the per serving line.

The nutrition information that appears with each recipe was submitted by the participating companies and associations. **Every effort has been made to check the accuracy of these numbers. However, because numerous variables account for a wide range of values for certain foods, all nutritive analyses that appear in this publication should be considered approximate.** For consistency, many of the figures in the nutrition charts have been rounded to the nearest whole number. The figures in the nutrition charts are based on the nutritive values for foods in the U.S. Department of Agriculture Composition of Foods Handbook No. 8 (series), or from values submitted directly by the food manufacturers themselves.

What This Publication Does and Does Not Do

These recipes were all selected to help you make smart choices about the desserts you want to enjoy. From elegant cakes to serve to guests, to quick and easy cookies for kids, you're sure to find low-calorie, low-fat desserts for almost any occasion.

This publication offers you a wide variety of recipes that are, on a per serving basis, lower in calories, fat, cholesterol and sodium than regular desserts. **The recipes in this publication are NOT intended as a medically therapeutic program, nor as a substitute for medically approved diet plans for people on cholesterol-, fat- or sodium-restricted diets. You should consult your physician before beginning any diet plan.** The recipes offered here can be part of a healthy lifestyle that meets recognized dietary guidelines. A healthy lifestyle includes not only eating a balanced diet, but engaging in appropriate exercise as well.

By preparing desserts that are low in calories, fat, cholesterol and sodium, you can actually enjoy your favorite part of the meal. And with the wonderful variety offered here, you don't have to sacrifice either flavor or convenience. So let yourself go and give in to guilt-free sweet indulgence!

Light & Luscious

CAKES

Peachy Chocolate Cake

No Cholesterol

Makes 12 servings

1½ cups all-purpose flour
1 cup sugar
¼ cup HERSHEY'S® Cocoa
1 teaspoon baking soda
½ teaspoon salt
1 cup water
¼ cup vegetable oil
1 tablespoon white vinegar
1 teaspoon vanilla extract
2 cups peeled, sliced fresh
    peaches, divided

Heat oven to 350°F. Grease and flour
two 8-inch round baking pans. In
large bowl, stir together flour, sugar,
cocoa, baking soda and salt. Add
water, oil, vinegar and vanilla. Beat
with wire whisk or spoon just until
batter is smooth and ingredients are
well blended. Pour into prepared
pans. Bake 20 to 25 minutes or until
wooden pick inserted in center comes
out clean. Cool 10 minutes; remove
from pans to wire racks. Cool
completely. Just before serving, place
one cake layer on serving plate;
arrange 1 cup of the peaches on layer.
Top with second cake layer and
remaining 1 cup peaches. Cut into
slices; serve immediately.

Nutrients per serving:

Calories	181	Sodium	181 mg
Fat	5 g	Cholesterol	0 mg

Della Robbia Cake

Della Robbia Cake

Under 200 Calories

Makes 12 servings

Cake

1 package DUNCAN HINES®
    Angel Food Cake Mix
1½ teaspoons grated lemon peel

Glaze

6 tablespoons sugar
1½ tablespoons cornstarch
1 cup water
1 tablespoon lemon juice
½ teaspoon vanilla extract
    Few drops red food coloring
6 cling peach slices
6 medium strawberries, sliced

1. Preheat oven to 375°F.

2. **For Cake,** prepare following
package directions adding lemon peel
with Cake Flour Mixture (red "B"
packet). Bake and cool following
package directions.

3. **For Glaze,** combine sugar,
cornstarch and water in small
saucepan. Cook on medium-high heat
until mixture thickens and is clear.
Remove from heat. Stir in lemon
juice, vanilla extract and red food
coloring.

4. Alternate peach slices with
strawberry slices around top of cooled
cake. Pour glaze over fruit and top of
cake. Refrigerate leftovers.

Nutrients per serving:

Calories	145	Sodium	100 mg
Fat	0 g	Cholesterol	0 mg

Lemony Light Vineyard "Cheesecakes"

Lemony Light Vineyard "Cheesecakes"

Under 100 Calories

Makes 6 servings

- 1 envelope unflavored gelatin
- ½ cup cold water
- 1 package (8 ounces) light cream cheese, softened
- 1 cup plain lowfat yogurt
- ⅓ cup sugar
- 1 tablespoon grated lemon peel
- 1 tablespoon lemon juice
- ¼ teaspoon vanilla
- 4 ice cubes
- 1½ cups seedless *or* halved, seeded Chilean grapes

In small saucepan, sprinkle gelatin over cold water; let stand 1 minute to soften. Warm over low heat to dissolve. Combine in blender softened gelatin, cream cheese, yogurt, sugar, lemon peel, lemon juice and vanilla. Blend until smooth, scraping sides as needed. Add ice cubes; blend until smooth. Divide grapes between six (6-ounce) custard cups or individual dessert dishes. Pour cheese mixture over each, dividing equally. Chill until set. Garnish with additional grated lemon peel, if desired.

Nutrients per serving:			
Calories	97	Sodium	141 mg
Fat	2 g	Cholesterol	6 mg

Favorite recipe from **Chilean Winter Fruit Association**

Chocolate Raspberry Cheesecake

Under 200 Calories

Makes 12 servings

- 3 squares BAKER'S® Semi-Sweet Chocolate
- ¼ cup water
- 1 (8 oz.) container PHILADELPHIA BRAND® LIGHT Pasteurized Process Cream Cheese Product
- ½ cup light or low calorie raspberry fruit spread, divided
- 3¼ cups (8 ounces) COOL WHIP LITE™ Whipped Topping, thawed, divided
- 2 tablespoons water
- 36 fresh raspberries
- 2 chocolate wafers, crushed

MICROWAVE° chocolate with ¼ cup water in large microwavable bowl at HIGH 1 to 1½ minutes until almost melted; stir until completely melted. (Mixture will be thick.)

BEAT chocolate, cream cheese product and ¼ cup of the fruit spread. Immediately stir in 2½ cups whipped topping until smooth. Spread in 8- or 9-inch pie plate or springform pan. Freeze 3 to 4 hours.

REMOVE from freezer; let stand 15 minutes. Briefly heat and stir remaining fruit spread and 2 tablespoons water until well blended. Remove from heat. Garnish each serving with fruit spread mixture, remaining whipped topping, raspberries and cookie crumbs. Store leftover cheesecake in freezer.

°*Range Top: Heat chocolate with water in saucepan over very low heat; stir constantly until just melted. Remove from heat; continue as above.*

Nutrients per serving:			
Calories	139	Sodium	135 mg
Fat	8 g	Cholesterol	10 mg

Tropical Fruit Delight

Low Sodium

Makes 16 servings

Cake

1 package DUNCAN HINES®
DeLights Lemon Cake Mix
½ cup CITRUS HILL® Orange
Juice
2 eggs
1 tablespoon grated orange
peel
Confectioners sugar

Topping

1 can (11 ounces) mandarin
orange segments,
undrained
1 can (8 ounces) crushed
pineapple with juice,
undrained
¼ cup granulated sugar
1 tablespoon cornstarch
1 tablespoon margarine or
butter (optional)
1 banana, sliced
¼ cup flaked coconut (optional)

1. Preheat oven to 350°F. Grease and
flour 10-inch Bundt® pan.

2. **For Cake**, empty mix into large
bowl. Add water to orange juice to
equal 1⅓ cups. Add orange juice
mixture, eggs and orange peel to mix.
Beat at medium speed with electric
mixer for 2 minutes. Bake and cool
following package directions. Sift
confectioners sugar over cooled cake.

3. **For Topping**, drain mandarin
oranges, reserving juice. Drain
pineapple, reserving juice. Combine
juices in 1 cup measure. Add water or
orange juice to fruit juices to equal 1
cup. Pour into small saucepan.
Combine granulated sugar and
cornstarch. Stir into liquid. Cook on
medium heat, stirring constantly, until
thickened. Add margarine, if desired.
Stir until melted. Cool.

4. Stir mandarin oranges, pineapple
and banana into cooled sauce. Cut
cake into 16 servings. Spoon sauce
over each serving. Sprinkle with
coconut, if desired.

Nutrients per serving:			
Calories	209	Sodium	228 mg
Fat	5 g	Cholesterol	53 mg

Tropical Fruit Delight

Blueberry Angel Food Cake Roll

Blueberry Angel Food Cake Rolls

Under 200 Calories

Makes 16 servings

**1 package DUNCAN HINES®
    Angel Food Cake Mix
    Confectioners sugar
1 can (21 ounces) blueberry pie
    filling
¼ cup confectioners sugar
    Mint leaves, for garnish
    (optional)**

1. Preheat oven to 350°F. Line two 15½×10½×1-inch jelly-roll pans with aluminum foil.

2. Prepare cake following package directions. Divide into pans. Spread evenly. Cut through batter with knife or spatula to remove large air bubbles. Bake at 350°F for 15 minutes or until set. Invert cakes at once onto clean, lint-free dishtowels dusted with confectioners sugar. Remove foil carefully. Roll up each cake with towel jelly-roll fashion, starting at short end. Cool completely.

3. Unroll cakes. Spread about 1 cup blueberry pie filling to within 1 inch of edges on each cake. Reroll and place seam-side down on serving plate. Dust with ¼ cup confectioners sugar. Garnish with mint leaves, if desired.

Nutrients per serving:

Calories	143	Sodium	77 mg
Fat	0 g	Cholesterol	0 mg

Harvest Bundt® Cake

Makes 16 servings

2½ cups all-purpose flour
1 tablespoon baking powder
2 teaspoons ground cinnamon
1½ teaspoons baking soda
1½ cups boiling water
1½ cups NABISCO® 100% Bran™
1 cup firmly packed light brown sugar
1 cup seedless raisins
½ cup margarine, melted
1 cup MOTT'S® Regular Apple Sauce
2 eggs, slightly beaten

In medium bowl, mix flour, baking powder, cinnamon and baking soda; set aside. In large separate bowl, combine water, bran, brown sugar, raisins and margarine; let stand 5 minutes. Stir in apple sauce, eggs and flour mixture. Spoon into greased and floured 12-cup Bundt® pan. Bake at 350°F for 55 to 65 minutes or until toothpick inserted in center comes out clean. Cool in pan 10 minutes. Remove from pan; cool on wire rack.

Nutrients per serving:

Calories	242	Sodium	272 mg
Fat	7 g	Cholesterol	27 mg

Light Mocha Cake with Raspberry Sauce

Makes 24 servings

2 cups all-purpose flour
1¼ cups granulated sugar
½ cup NESTLÉ® Cocoa
2 teaspoons baking soda
1 teaspoon baking powder
½ teaspoon salt
1 cup buttermilk
1 cup hot coffee
⅔ cup vegetable oil
1 teaspoon vanilla extract
Confectioners' sugar
Raspberry Sauce (recipe follows)
Low-calorie whipped topping, optional

Preheat oven to 350°F. Grease and flour 13×9-inch baking pan. In large mixer bowl, combine flour, granulated sugar, cocoa, baking soda, baking powder and salt. Gradually beat in buttermilk, coffee, oil and vanilla extract; continue beating until well blended. Pour into prepared pan.

Bake 35 to 40 minutes or until wooden toothpick inserted in center comes out clean. Cool completely. Sprinkle with confectioners' sugar. Cut into 24 squares. Top with cooled Raspberry Sauce and whipped topping.

Raspberry Sauce: In blender or food processor, purée one 10-oz. pkg. frozen raspberries, thawed, until smooth. Press through fine sieve to remove seeds. In small saucepan, combine ½ cup water and 2 tablespoons cornstarch. Stir in purée. Bring to a boil over medium heat, stirring constantly. Boil 1 minute, stirring constantly. Cool.

Nutrients per serving:

Calories	156	Sodium	139 mg
Fat	6 g	Cholesterol	0 mg

Light 'n Luscious Cheesecake

Low Cholesterol

Makes 8 servings

- 1 tablespoon graham cracker crumbs
- 1 cup (8 ounces) lowfat cottage cheese
- 1 cup (8 ounces) plain lowfat yogurt
- ½ cup HELLMANN'S® or BEST FOODS® Light or Cholesterol Free Reduced Calorie Mayonnaise
- ⅓ cup sugar
- 2 teaspoons grated lemon peel
- 1 tablespoon lemon juice
- 1 teaspoon vanilla
- 2 egg whites
  Raspberry Sauce (recipe follows)
  Fresh raspberries for garnish (optional)
  Additional graham cracker crumbs (optional)

Grease 8-inch springform pan; dust with graham cracker crumbs. In blender or food processor container spoon cottage cheese. Process until smooth. Add yogurt, mayonnaise, sugar, lemon peel, lemon juice and vanilla; process until smooth. Add egg whites; process until well mixed. Pour into prepared pan. Bake in 325°F oven 30 minutes. *Turn off oven.* Leave cheesecake in oven with door ajar 30 minutes. Cool in pan on wire rack. Cover; chill several hours. Before serving, remove side of pan. Serve with Raspberry Sauce. If desired, garnish with fresh raspberries and additional graham cracker crumbs.

Raspberry Sauce: In blender or food processor, purée 1 package (10 ounces) frozen raspberries, thawed; strain. Stir in ⅓ cup Karo® Light or Dark Corn Syrup. *Makes about 2½ cups.*

Nutrients per serving:

Calories	209	Sodium	313 mg
Fat	5 g	Cholesterol	9 mg

Golden Apple Cupcakes

Under 200 Calories

Makes 24 cupcakes

- 1 (18- to 20-ounce) package yellow cake mix
- 1 cup MOTT'S® Chunky Apple Sauce
- ⅓ cup vegetable oil
- 3 eggs
- ¼ cup firmly packed light brown sugar
- ¼ cup chopped walnuts
- ½ teaspoon ground cinnamon

In bowl, combine cake mix, apple sauce, oil and eggs; blend according to package directions. Spoon batter into 24 paper-lined muffin-pan cups. Mix brown sugar, walnuts and cinnamon; sprinkle over batter. Bake at 350°F for 20 to 25 minutes or until toothpick inserted in center comes out clean. Cool in pan 10 minutes. Remove from pan; cool on wire rack.

Nutrients per cupcake:

Calories	157	Sodium	146 mg
Fat	6 g	Cholesterol	27 mg

Light 'n Luscious Cheesecake

Carrot Pudding Cake with Lemon Sauce

Carrot Pudding Cake with Lemon Sauce

No Cholesterol

Makes 8 servings

¼ cup liquid vegetable oil
   margarine
⅓ cup firmly packed brown
   sugar
½ cup frozen apple juice
   concentrate, thawed
3 egg whites, slightly beaten
1 cup QUAKER® Oat Bran hot
   cereal, uncooked
½ cup all-purpose flour
2 teaspoons baking powder
1 teaspoon ground cinnamon
2 cups shredded carrots (about
   4 or 5 medium)
½ cup granulated sugar
4 teaspoons cornstarch
1 cup hot water
1 tablespoon liquid vegetable
   oil margarine
1 tablespoon lemon juice
½ teaspoon grated lemon peel
1 drop yellow food coloring
   (optional)

Heat oven to 325°F. Lightly spray 1½- or 2-qt. casserole with no-stick cooking spray or oil lightly. Combine ¼ cup margarine and brown sugar. Add apple juice concentrate and egg whites, mixing well. Add combined oat bran, flour, baking powder and cinnamon; mix well. Stir in carrots; pour into prepared dish. Bake 45 to 50 minutes or until edges are lightly browned and center is firm. Cool on wire rack about 1 hour.

Combine granulated sugar and cornstarch. Gradually add water, mixing until sugar dissolves. Cook over medium heat about 3 minutes, stirring constantly or until thickened and clear. Remove from heat; stir in remaining ingredients. Spoon 2 tablespoons lemon sauce over each serving.

Microwave Lemon Sauce Directions:
In 4-cup microwavable measuring cup, combine granulated sugar and cornstarch. Gradually add water, mixing until sugar dissolves. Microwave at HIGH 2 to 3 minutes or until sauce is clear and thickened, stirring after every minute. Add remaining ingredients, mixing well. Cool slightly.

Nutrients per serving:

Calories	270	Sodium	200 mg
Fat	8 g	Cholesterol	0 mg

Tropical Banana Cake

Makes 16 servings

½ cup CRISCO® Shortening
1¾ cups sugar
2 eggs
1 egg white
½ cup skim milk
1½ teaspoons vanilla
1 cup mashed banana (about 2 medium)
1 can (8 ounces) crushed pineapple in unsweetened pineapple juice, undrained
3 cups all-purpose flour
1¼ teaspoons ground cinnamon
1 teaspoon baking soda
½ teaspoon salt
1 tablespoon finely chopped pecans

1. Heat oven to 350°F. Oil and flour 10-inch tube pan.

2. Combine Crisco® and sugar in large bowl. Beat at medium speed of electric mixer until blended. Add eggs and egg white. Beat until light and fluffy. Add milk, vanilla, banana and pineapple with juice. Beat at low speed until mixed. (Batter will appear slightly curdled.)

3. Combine flour, cinnamon, baking soda and salt in separate bowl. Add to creamed mixture. Beat at low speed until mixed. Pour into pan. Sprinkle with nuts.

4. Bake at 350°F for 1 hour 10 minutes or until wooden pick inserted near center comes out clean. Cool in pan 25 minutes. Remove from pan. Cool completely on rack.

Nutrients per serving:

Calories	251	Sodium	134 mg
Fat	7 g	Cholesterol	27 mg

Chocolate Angel Food Cake

Makes 12 servings

One 14.5-oz to 16-oz. pkg. angel food cake mix, plus ingredients to prepare mix
½ cup NESTLÉ® Cocoa
Confectioners' sugar, for garnish
Strawberries, optional

Preheat oven according to cake mix directions. Combine cake mix (or cake flour) and cocoa. Prepare, bake and cool angel food cake according to cake mix directions. Sift confectioners' sugar over top of cake; serve with strawberries, if desired.

Nutrients per serving:

Calories	157	Sodium	142 mg
Fat	1 g	Cholesterol	0 mg

Chocolate Angel Food Cake

Banana Upside-Down Cake

Low Cholesterol

Makes 9 servings

3 tablespoons margarine
½ cup brown sugar, packed
4 firm, medium DOLE®
    Bananas, peeled, divided
1 egg
½ cup granulated sugar
3 tablespoons vegetable oil
2 tablespoons milk
1 teaspoon vanilla extract
½ teaspoon DOLE® Orange zest
1 cup all-purpose flour
1 teaspoon baking powder
½ teaspoon ground cinnamon
¼ teaspoon baking soda
⅛ teaspoon salt

- Melt margarine in 9-inch square cake pan 2 to 3 minutes as oven preheats to 350°F. Remove pan from oven; stir in brown sugar.

- Slice 3 of the bananas; arrange in single layer in brown sugar mixture. Cut remaining banana in chunks. Place banana chunks, egg, granulated sugar, oil, milk, vanilla and orange zest in food processor or blender. Process until smooth.

- Combine flour, baking powder, cinnamon, baking soda and salt in large bowl. Add banana mixture to dry mixture. Stir until blended. Pour batter over bananas in cake pan.

- Bake in 350°F oven 30 minutes or until cake tester inserted in center comes out clean. Cool in pan on wire rack 5 minutes. Invert onto serving plate. Serve warm or cool.

Nutrients per serving:

Calories	271	Sodium	137 mg
Fat	9 g	Cholesterol	31 mg

Raspberry Shortcake

Under 200 Calories

Makes 8 servings

1½ cups whole frozen
    raspberries, divided
4½ tablespoons sugar, divided
1 cup all-purpose flour
1 teaspoon baking powder
¼ teaspoon baking soda
1 tablespoon margarine
1 egg white
⅓ cup evaporated skim milk
¼ teaspoon almond extract
¾ cup low-fat cottage cheese
1½ teaspoons sugar
1 teaspoon lemon juice

Preheat oven to 450°F. Spray baking sheet with non-stick cooking spray. In small bowl, toss 1¼ cups of the raspberries with 2½ tablespoons sugar; refrigerate. In medium bowl, stir together flour, baking powder, baking soda and remaining 2 tablespoons sugar. Cut in margarine using pastry blender or 2 knives. In separate bowl, beat egg white, evaporated skim milk and extract. Add to dry ingredients. Mix lightly. Knead slightly on lightly floured board. Roll out to ½-inch thickness. Use 2½-inch biscuit cutter to cut out 8 biscuits. Place biscuits on prepared baking sheet and bake for 10 minutes or until slightly brown on top. Meanwhile, in food processor or blender, process cottage cheese, 1½ teaspoons sugar and lemon juice. Fold in remaining ¼ cup raspberries. Split each warm biscuit in half. Place bottom halves in each of 8 individual serving dishes. Top with half the cottage cheese mixture and reserved sugared raspberries. Top with remaining biscuit halves, cottage cheese mixture and raspberries.

Nutrients per serving:

Calories	166	Sodium	190 mg
Fat	2 g	Cholesterol	1 mg

Favorite recipe from **The Sugar Association**

Mini Almond Cheesecake

Mini Almond Cheesecakes

Under 200 Calories

Makes 12 servings

¾ cup ground almonds
1 tablespoon PARKAY® Margarine, melted
1 envelope unflavored gelatin
¼ cup cold water
1 (12-oz.) container PHILADELPHIA BRAND® LIGHT Pasteurized Process Cream Cheese Product
¾ cup skim milk
½ cup sugar or 12 packets sugar substitute
¼ teaspoon almond extract
3 cups peeled peach slices

- Stir together almonds and margarine in small bowl. Press mixture evenly onto bottoms of twelve paper-lined baking cups.

- Soften gelatin in water in small saucepan; stir over low heat until dissolved.

- Beat cream cheese product, milk, sugar and almond extract in large mixing bowl at medium speed with electric mixer until well blended. Stir in gelatin. Pour into baking cups; freeze until firm.

- Place peaches in food processor or blender container; process until smooth. Spoon peach purée onto individual plates.

- Remove cheesecakes from freezer 10 minutes before serving. Peel off paper. Invert cheesecakes onto plates. Garnish with additional peach slices, raspberries and fresh mint leaves, if desired.

Note: For a sweeter peach purée, add sugar to taste.

Nutrients per serving:

Calories	175	Sodium	180 mg
Fat	10 g	Cholesterol	11 mg

Orange Poppy Seed Cake

Low Sodium

Makes 16 servings

1 (8 oz.) container
   **PHILADELPHIA BRAND®
   LIGHT Pasteurized Process
   Cream Cheese Product**
⅓ cup **PARKAY® Margarine**
1 cup sugar
3 eggs, separated
2 cups flour
1 teaspoon **CALUMET® Baking
   Powder**
1 teaspoon baking soda
1 cup **BREAKSTONE'S®
   LIGHT CHOICE® Sour
   Half and Half**
2 tablespoons poppy seeds
1 tablespoon grated orange
   peel
½ cup sugar or 12 packets sugar
   substitute
½ cup orange juice
3 tablespoons powdered sugar

• Preheat oven to 350°.

• Beat cream cheese product,
   margarine and 1 cup sugar in large
   mixing bowl at medium speed with
   electric mixer until well blended.
   Add egg yolks, one at a time, mixing
   well after each addition.

• Mix together flour, baking powder
   and baking soda; add to cream
   cheese mixture alternately with sour
   half and half. Stir in poppy seeds
   and orange peel.

• Beat egg whites in small mixing
   bowl at high speed with electric
   mixer until stiff peaks form; fold
   into cream cheese mixture. Pour
   into greased 10-inch fluted
   tube pan.

• Bake 50 minutes.

• Stir together ½ cup sugar and
   orange juice in saucepan over low
   heat until sugar dissolves. Prick hot
   cake several times with fork. Pour
   syrup over cake; cool 10 minutes.
   Invert onto serving plate. Cool
   completely. Sprinkle with powdered
   sugar. Garnish with quartered
   orange slices, if desired.

Nutrients per serving:

Calories	228	Sodium	157 mg
Fat	9 g	Cholesterol	48 mg

Angel Food Cake with Blueberry Yogurt Sauce

Under 200 Calories

Makes 4 servings

½ cup frozen blueberries
1 small prepared angel food
   cake
½ cup non-fat vanilla yogurt
1 tablespoon sugar
1 teaspoon lemon juice

Set blueberries out to thaw slightly.
Cut angel food cake into 4 slices. In
small bowl, stir together yogurt, sugar
and lemon juice. To serve, top each
slice of cake with 2 tablespoons sauce
and 2 tablespoons blueberries.

Nutrients per serving:

Calories	163	Sodium	291 mg
Fat	0 g	Cholesterol	0 mg

Favorite recipe from **The Sugar Association**

Orange Poppy Seed Cake

Creamy Citrus Cheesecake

Makes 8 servings

- ¾ cup crushed graham crackers
- 2 tablespoons margarine, melted
- 3 eggs
- ½ cup sugar
- 1 teaspoon finely shredded orange peel
- ¼ cup orange juice
- 3 teaspoons vanilla, divided
- 2 (8-ounce) packages light cream cheese
- 1 cup DANNON® Plain, Lemon or Vanilla Lowfat Yogurt, divided
- 2 tablespoons confectioners sugar

In bowl, combine graham crackers and margarine. Press onto bottom of 7- or 8-inch springform pan. Bake at 325° for 6 minutes; let cool.

In blender, combine eggs, sugar, orange peel, orange juice and 2 teaspoons of the vanilla. Cut cream cheese into chunks; add to mixture and blend until smooth. Stir in ½ cup of the yogurt. Pour into crust. Bake at 325° for 50 to 60 minutes or until nearly set.

Combine remaining ½ cup yogurt, confectioners sugar and remaining 1 teaspoon vanilla. Spread over hot cheesecake. Loosen sides of pan. Cool on wire rack. Chill before serving. Garnish with orange peel, if desired.

Nutrients per serving:

Calories	186	Sodium	286 mg
Fat	8 g	Cholesterol	88 mg

Creamy Citrus Cheesecake

Apple Chiffon Cake

Under 200 Calories

Makes 12 servings

Cake

⅓ cup CRISCO® PURITAN® Oil
¾ cup sugar
2 eggs
¾ cup all-purpose flour
½ teaspoon baking powder
¼ teaspoon salt
¼ teaspoon baking soda
¼ teaspoon ground nutmeg
¼ teaspoon ground ginger
1 cup finely chopped peeled
   apples (2 small to medium)

Topping

2 tablespoons sugar
2 tablespoons finely chopped
   walnuts
½ teaspoon ground cinnamon

1. Heat oven to 350°F.

2. **For Cake,** combine Crisco®
Puritan® Oil and sugar in large bowl.
Beat at medium speed of electric
mixer until mixed. Add eggs; beat
well.

3. Combine flour, baking powder,
salt, baking soda, nutmeg and ginger
in small bowl. Add to oil mixture.
Beat just until blended. Stir in apples.
Spread in ungreased 9-inch
square pan.

4. **For Topping,** combine sugar, nuts
and cinnamon in small bowl. Sprinkle
over batter. Bake at 350°F for 25 to
30 minutes or until wooden pick
inserted in center comes out clean.
Cut into 3×2¼-inch rectangles. Serve
warm or at room temperature.

Nutrients per serving:

Calories	162	Sodium	86 mg
Fat	8 g	Cholesterol	36 mg

Chocolate Orange Delight

Under 200 Calories

Makes 16 servings

Cake

1 tablespoon grated orange
   peel
1 package DUNCAN HINES®
   DeLights Devil's Food
   Cake Mix

Topping

1 container (8 ounces) frozen
   whipped topping, thawed
2 tablespoons CITRUS HILL®
   Frozen Orange Juice
   Concentrate, thawed
Orange slices, for garnish

1. Preheat oven to 350°F. Grease and
flour 13×9×2-inch pan.

2. **For Cake,** add orange peel to mix.
Prepare, bake and cool following
package directions.

3. **For Topping,** combine whipped
topping and orange juice concentrate
in medium bowl. Stir until blended.
Spoon dollop of topping on each cake
serving. Garnish with orange slices.
Refrigerate leftover topping.

*Tip: To make orange juice
from remaining concentrate, measure
remaining concentrate; add 3 times
the amount of water to concentrate.*

Nutrients per serving:

Calories	193	Sodium	271 mg
Fat	7 g	Cholesterol	52 mg

Pleasing

◇◆◇

PIES

Deep-Dish Peach Pie

Makes 8 servings

Pastry for 1-crust pie°
1 cup sugar
2 tablespoons cornstarch
3 pounds peaches, seeded,
   pared and sliced (about
   6 cups)
2 tablespoons REALEMON®
   Lemon Juice from
   Concentrate
1 tablespoon margarine, melted
¼ teaspoon almond extract
2 tablespoons sliced almonds

Preheat oven to 375°. Remove and
reserve *1 tablespoon* sugar. In small
bowl, combine remaining sugar and
cornstarch. In large bowl, toss
peaches with ReaLemon® brand; add
sugar mixture, margarine and extract.
Turn into 8-inch square baking dish.
Roll pastry to 9-inch square; cut slits
near center. Place pastry over filling;
turn under edges, seal and flute.
Sprinkle with reserved *1 tablespoon*
sugar and almonds. Bake 45 to 50
minutes or until golden brown.

°*Cholesterol analysis based on pastry
made with vegetable shortening or
margarine.*

Nutrients per serving:

Calories	292	Sodium	163 mg
Fat	10 g	Cholesterol	0 mg

Iced Coffee and Chocolate Pie

Makes 8 servings

¼ cup cold skim milk
2 envelopes unflavored gelatin
1 cup skim milk, heated to
   boiling
2 cups vanilla ice milk
⅓ cup sugar
2 tablespoons instant coffee
   granules
1 teaspoon vanilla extract
1 (6-ounce) KEEBLER® Ready-
   Crust® Chocolate Flavored
   Pie Crust
Reduced calorie whipped
   topping, optional
Chocolate curls, optional

In blender container, add ¼ cup cold
milk. Sprinkle gelatin over milk and
mix on LOW. Let stand 3 to 4
minutes to soften. Add hot milk;
cover and mix on LOW until gelatin
dissolves, about 2 minutes. Add ice
milk, sugar, coffee granules and
vanilla. Cover and mix until smooth.
Pour into crust. Chill at least 2 hours.
Garnish with whipped topping and
chocolate curls, if desired.

Nutrients per serving:

Calories	220	Sodium	210 mg
Fat	6 g	Cholesterol	6 mg

Deep-Dish Peach Pie

Fruit Lover's Tart

Low Cholesterol

Makes 8 servings

1¼ cups QUAKER® Oats (Quick
   or Old Fashioned,
   uncooked)
⅓ cup firmly packed brown
   sugar
¼ cup all-purpose flour
2 tablespoons margarine,
   melted
2 egg whites
1 cup (8 ounces) part-skim
   ricotta cheese
¼ cup (2 ounces) light cream
   cheese, softened
2 tablespoons powdered sugar
½ teaspoon grated lemon peel
4½ cups any combination sliced
   fresh or frozen fruit,
   thawed, well drained

Heat oven to 350°F. Lightly spray
9-inch pie plate with no-stick cooking
spray or oil lightly. Combine oats,
brown sugar, flour, margarine and egg
whites, mixing until moistened. Press
mixture onto bottom of prepared
plate. Bake 15 to 18 minutes or until
light golden brown. Remove to wire
rack; cool completely. Combine
cheeses, powdered sugar and lemon
peel. Spread onto oat base; top with
fruit. Chill 2 hours.

Microwave Directions:
Combine oats, brown sugar, flour,
margarine and egg whites, mixing
until moistened. Press mixture onto
bottom of 9-inch microwave-safe pie
plate. Microwave on HIGH 2 minutes
30 seconds to 3 minutes or until top
springs back when lightly touched.
Cool completely. Proceed as above.

Nutrients per serving:

Calories	240	Sodium	110 mg
Fat	8 g	Cholesterol	15 mg

Cherry Yogurt Sesame Pie

Low Sodium

Makes 8 servings

Crust
1 cup all-purpose flour
2 tablespoons wheat germ
2 tablespoons sesame seeds
1 tablespoon sugar
⅓ cup butter or margarine
4 tablespoons cold water

Filling
1 envelope unflavored gelatin
¼ cup cold water
1 carton (8 ounces) nonfat plain
   or lowfat vanilla yogurt
1 can (21 ounces) cherry pie
   filling and topping

For Crust, place flour, wheat germ,
sesame seeds and sugar in large
mixing bowl. Cut in butter until
mixture is size of small peas. Add 4
tablespoons water and mix with fork
until dough just holds together. Form
into a ball; flatten and roll out on
floured surface to fit 9-inch pie pan.
Fit dough into pan, flute edges and
prick crust several times with fork.
Bake at 450°F for 10 to 15 minutes or
until golden brown. Cool completely.

For Filling, in large microwave-safe
bowl, sprinkle gelatin over ¼ cup
water; let stand 1 minute to soften.
Microwave on full power (high) 10
seconds; stir until gelatin is dissolved.
Whisk in yogurt, then gently fold in
cherry pie filling. Spoon into cooled
baked crust. Chill until firm, about 2
hours.

Nutrients per serving:

Calories	245	Sodium	104 mg
Fat	9 g	Cholesterol	22 mg

Favorite recipe from **New York Cherry
Growers Association**

Lovely Lemon Cheese Pie

Lovely Lemon Cheese Pie

Under 200 Calories

Makes 8 servings

1 whole graham cracker,
    crushed, *or* 2 tablespoons
    graham cracker crumbs,
    divided
1 package (4-serving size)
    JELL-O® Brand Lemon
    Flavor Sugar Free Gelatin
⅔ cup boiling water
1 cup 1% lowfat cottage cheese
1 container (8 ounces)
    pasteurized process cream
    cheese product
2 cups thawed COOL WHIP
    LITE™ Whipped Topping
1 cup reduced-calorie cherry
    pie filling

• Spray 9-inch pie plate or 8- or 9-inch springform pan lightly with non-stick cooking spray. Sprinkle sides with half of the graham cracker crumbs. (If desired, omit graham cracker crumb garnish; sprinkle bottom of pan with remaining graham cracker crumbs.)

• Completely dissolve gelatin in boiling water; pour into blender container. Add cottage cheese and cream cheese product; cover. Blend at medium speed, scraping down sides occasionally, about 2 minutes or until mixture is completely smooth. Pour into large mixing bowl. Gently stir in whipped topping. Pour into prepared pan; smooth top. Sprinkle the remaining crumbs around outside edge. Chill until set, about 4 hours.

• When ready to serve, top with pie filling.

Nutrients per serving:			
Calories	160	Sodium	330 mg
Fat	7 g	Cholesterol	15 mg

Easy Pineapple Pie

Cranberry-Apple Tart

Makes 9 servings

Crust
> 3 cups RALSTON® Brand Fruit
> & Nut Muesli with
> Cranberries, crushed to
> 2 cups
> ¼ cup (½ stick) margarine or
> butter, melted
> ¼ cup packed brown sugar

Filling
> 2 cups cranberries, fresh or
> frozen
> ½ cup granulated sugar
> ½ cup water
> 1 tablespoon lemon juice
> 1 can (20 ounces) apple pie
> filling
> Shredded cheese and mint
> leaves, optional

To prepare Crust: Preheat oven to
350°. In medium bowl combine
cereal, margarine and brown sugar.
Press cereal mixture firmly into
9-inch fluted tart pan or 9-inch pie
plate. Bake 7 to 8 minutes or until
lightly browned. Cool completely.

To prepare Filling: In medium
saucepan over medium heat combine
cranberries, granulated sugar, water
and lemon juice. Cook, stirring
frequently, until mixture comes to a
boil; reduce heat and simmer 15 to 18
minutes, stirring frequently. Remove
from heat and cool completely. Pour
apple pie filling into cooled crust; top
with cooled cranberry mixture.
Garnish with cheese and mint if
desired.

Nutrients per serving:

Calories	288	Sodium	185 mg
Fat	7 g	Cholesterol	0 mg

Easy Pineapple Pie

Makes 6 to 8 servings

> 1 can (20 ounces) DOLE®
> Crushed Pineapple in
> Syrup°
> 1 package (3.5 ounces) instant
> lemon pudding and pie
> filling mix
> 1 cup milk
> 1 carton (4 ounces) frozen
> whipped topping, thawed
> 2 tablespoons DOLE® Lemon
> juice
> 1 teaspoon DOLE® Lemon zest
> 1 (8- or 9-inch) graham cracker
> pie crust

- Drain pineapple well. Combine
pudding mix and milk in medium
bowl. Beat 2 to 3 minutes until very
thick.

- Fold in whipped topping,
pineapple, lemon juice and lemon
zest. Pour into crust. Cover and
refrigerate 4 hours or overnight.
Garnish as desired.

°*Use pineapple packed in juice, if
desired.*

Nutrients per serving:

Calories	266	Sodium	321 mg
Fat	10 g	Cholesterol	2 mg

Light Lemon Meringue Pie

Makes 8 servings

Crust

1¼ cups all-purpose flour
½ teaspoon salt (optional)
⅓ cup CRISCO® Shortening
¼ cup CITRUS HILL® Orange
Juice

Filling

1 cup sugar
⅓ cup cornstarch
⅛ teaspoon salt (optional)
1½ cups cold water
1 egg yolk, lightly beaten
1 teaspoon grated fresh lemon
peel
⅓ cup fresh lemon juice

Meringue

3 egg whites
⅛ teaspoon salt (optional)
¼ cup sugar
½ teaspoon vanilla

1. Heat oven to 425°F.

2. **For Crust,** combine flour and salt (if used) in bowl. Cut in Crisco using pastry blender or 2 knives until all flour is blended in to form pea-sized chunks. Sprinkle orange juice over flour mixture 1 tablespoon at a time. Toss lightly with fork until dough forms. (Dough may seem slightly dry and crumbly.) Press into ball.

3. Press dough ball to form 5- to 6-inch "pancake." Roll between sheets of waxed paper until 1 inch larger than upside-down 9-inch pie plate. Peel off top sheet. Flip into pie plate. Remove other sheet. Fold dough edge under and flute. Prick bottom and sides with fork (50 times) to prevent shrinkage. Bake at 425°F for 10 to 15 minutes or until lightly browned.

4. **For Filling,** combine sugar, cornstarch and salt (if used) in heavy saucepan. Stir in water gradually, blending until smooth. Cook on medium-high heat, stirring constantly, until filling comes to a boil. Cook on medium heat, stirring constantly, 5 minutes. Remove from heat.

5. Stir small amount of hot mixture into egg yolk. Return mixture to saucepan. Cook, stirring, 1 minute. Remove from heat. Stir in lemon peel and juice. *Reduce oven temperature to 350°F.*

6. **For Meringue,** beat egg whites and salt (if used) until frothy. Add sugar gradually, beating well after each addition. Continue beating until stiff but not dry. Fold in vanilla.

7. Spoon filling into baked pie crust. Spread meringue over filling, sealing meringue to edge of pie crust. Bake at 350°F for 15 minutes or until golden brown. Cool completely on wire rack. Cut with sharp knife dipped in hot water.

Nutrients per serving (with optional salt):

Calories	289	Sodium	224 mg
Fat	9 g	Cholesterol	27 mg

Nutrients per serving (without optional salt):

Calories	289	Sodium	24 mg
Fat	9 g	Cholesterol	27 mg

Picnic Fruit Tart

Under 200 Calories

Makes 12 to 14 servings

¾ cup flour
¼ cup oat bran
2 tablespoons sugar
¼ cup PARKAY® Margarine
2 to 3 tablespoons cold water
1 envelope unflavored gelatin
½ cup cold water
1 (8 oz.) container
   PHILADELPHIA BRAND®
   LIGHT Pasteurized
   Process Cream Cheese
   Product
¼ cup sugar or 6 packets sugar
   substitute
1 teaspoon grated lemon peel
¼ cup skim milk
⅔ cup KRAFT® Apricot
   Preserves
¾ cup grape halves
¾ cup plum slices

• Preheat oven to 375°.

• Mix together flour, oat bran and 2 tablespoons sugar in medium bowl; cut in margarine until mixture resembles coarse crumbs. Sprinkle with 2 to 3 tablespoons water, mixing lightly with fork until just moistened. Roll into ball. Cover; chill.

• Roll out dough to 11-inch circle on lightly floured surface. Place in 9-inch tart pan with removable bottom. Trim edges; prick bottom with fork. Bake 16 to 18 minutes or until golden brown; cool.

• Soften gelatin in ½ cup cold water in small saucepan; stir over low heat until dissolved. Cool.

• Beat cream cheese product, ¼ cup sugar and lemon peel in large mixing bowl at medium speed with electric mixer until well blended. Gradually add gelatin and milk, mixing until well blended. Pour into crust. Chill until firm.

• Heat preserves in small saucepan over low heat until thinned. Spread evenly over tart. Arrange fruit over preserves. Carefully remove rim of pan.

Variation: To make individual tarts, prepare dough as directed. Divide dough into 14 equal portions; roll each into ball. Cover; chill. Roll each ball on lightly floured surface into 5-inch circle. Place in 3-inch tart pans; prick bottoms with fork. Bake 12 to 15 minutes or until lightly browned; cool. Continue as directed.

Nutrients per serving:

Calories	150	Sodium	130 mg
Fat	6 g	Cholesterol	10 mg

Frozen Yogurt Pie

Low Cholesterol

Makes 8 servings

1¾ cups NABISCO® 100%
   Bran™, finely rolled
¼ cup firmly packed brown
   sugar
⅓ cup margarine, melted
1½ pints vanilla frozen lowfat
   yogurt, softened
1½ cups MOTT'S® Chunky Apple
   Sauce
½ teaspoon ground cinnamon
   Fresh fruit and mint sprigs
   for garnish, optional

In small bowl, combine bran, brown sugar and margarine. Press mixture on bottom and side of 9-inch pie plate. Bake at 375°F for 8 minutes; cool completely. In large bowl, blend frozen yogurt, apple sauce and cinnamon. Spread in cooled crust. Freeze 4 hours or until firm. Garnish with fruit and mint if desired.

Nutrients per serving:

Calories	249	Sodium	232 mg
Fat	9 g	Cholesterol	4 mg

Picnic Fruit Tart

Pear Bistro Tart

Pear Bistro Tart

Low Sodium

Makes 10 servings

½ cup sugar
¼ cup cornstarch
2 eggs, slightly beaten
2 cups low-fat milk
1 teaspoon lemon zest
¼ teaspoon orange extract
    Baked 9-inch tart shell
2 fresh California Bartlett
    pears, pared, sliced
¼ cup apricot preserves, heated

Mix sugar and cornstarch in medium bowl; whisk in eggs. Scald milk; slowly whisk hot milk into egg mixture. Return to heat. Stir while cooking until thickened. Stir in lemon zest and orange extract; cool. Pour into baked tart shell. Arrange sliced pears on top; brush with hot apricot preserves. Garnish as desired.

Nutrients per serving:

Calories	214	Sodium	184 mg
Fat	8 g	Cholesterol	57 mg

Favorite recipe from **California Tree Fruit Agreement**

Luscious Pumpkin Pie

Makes 8 servings

1 teaspoon water
1 egg white
1 (6-ounce) KEEBLER® Ready-
    Crust® Pie Crust, Graham
    or Butter
2 eggs
1½ cups pumpkin pie filling
8 ounces DANNON® Plain
    Lowfat Yogurt
1 cup evaporated milk
¾ cup sugar
1 teaspoon vanilla extract
1 teaspoon ground cinnamon
¼ teaspoon ground cloves
¼ teaspoon ground ginger
¼ teaspoon ground nutmeg

Beat together water and egg white. Brush onto Keebler® Ready-Crust®. Place on cookie sheet and bake 3 minutes in 375° oven. Crust should be lightly golden. Cool thoroughly.

In a large bowl, slightly beat 2 eggs. Add pumpkin pie filling, yogurt, evaporated milk, sugar, vanilla, cinnamon, cloves, ginger and nutmeg. Stir until thoroughly mixed.

Pour into pie crust. Place on cookie sheet and bake 60 minutes in 375° oven or until set. Cool completely. Serve with whipped cream if desired.

Nutrients per serving:

Calories	289	Sodium	327 mg
Fat	10 g	Cholesterol	64 mg

Cranberry Apple Pie with Soft Gingersnap Crust

Under 200 Calories

Makes 8 servings

20 gingersnap cookies
1½ tablespoons margarine
2 McIntosh apples, pared and cored
1 cup fresh cranberries
5 tablespoons dark brown sugar
¼ teaspoon vanilla extract
¼ teaspoon ground cinnamon
1 teaspoon granulated sugar

Preheat oven to 375°F. Place gingersnaps and margarine in food processor; process until finely ground. Press gingersnap mixture into 8-inch pie plate. Bake 5 to 8 minutes; remove and cool crust. Chop apples in food processor. Add cranberries, brown sugar, vanilla and cinnamon; pulse just until mixed. Spoon apple-cranberry filling into another 8-inch pie plate or casserole dish. Sprinkle with granulated sugar. Bake 35 minutes or until tender. Spoon filling into gingersnap crust and serve immediately.

Nutrients per serving:

Calories	124	Sodium	90 mg
Fat	3 g	Cholesterol	0 mg

Favorite recipe from **The Sugar Association**

Fresh Fruit Tart

Low Cholesterol

Makes 8 servings

3 cups cooked rice
¼ cup sugar
1 egg, beaten
Vegetable cooking spray
1 package (8 ounces) light cream cheese, softened
¼ cup plain nonfat yogurt
¼ cup confectioner's sugar
1 teaspoon vanilla extract
⅓ cup low-sugar apricot or peach spread
1 tablespoon water
2 to 3 cups fresh fruit (sliced strawberries, raspberries, blueberries, sliced kiwifruit, grape halves)

Combine rice, sugar, and egg in medium bowl. Press into 12-inch pizza pan or 10-inch pie pan coated with cooking spray. Bake at 350°F. for 10 minutes. Cool.

Beat cream cheese and yogurt in medium bowl until light and fluffy. Add confectioner's sugar and vanilla; beat until well blended. Spread over crust.

Heat apricot spread and water in small saucepan over low heat. Strain; cool. Brush half of glaze over filling. Arrange fruit attractively over filling, starting at outer edge. Brush remaining glaze evenly over fruit. Cover and chill 1 to 2 hours before serving.

Nutrients per serving:

Calories	257	Sodium	432 mg
Fat	8 g	Cholesterol	48 mg

Favorite recipe from **USA Rice Council**

Bread Basket

◇◇◇◇

TREATS

Nutty Blueberry Muffins

No Cholesterol

Makes 8 large or 12 medium muffins

**1 package DUNCAN HINES®
    Blueberry Muffin Mix
2 egg whites
½ cup water
⅓ cup chopped pecans**

1. Preheat oven to 400°F. Grease 2½-inch muffin cups (or use paper liners).

2. Rinse blueberries from Mix with cold water and drain.

3. Empty muffin mix into bowl. Break up any lumps. Add egg whites and water. Stir until moistened, about 50 strokes. Stir in nuts; fold in blueberries.

4. For large muffins, fill cups two-thirds full. Bake at 400°F for 17 to 22 minutes or until toothpick inserted in center comes out clean. (For medium muffins, fill cups half full. Bake at 400°F for 15 to 20 minutes.) Cool 5 to 10 minutes. Loosen carefully before removing from pan. Serve warm.

Nutrients per muffin (for 8 large):

Calories	202	Sodium	284 mg
Fat	6 g	Cholesterol	0 mg

Nutrients per muffin (for 12 medium):

Calories	135	Sodium	189 mg
Fat	4 g	Cholesterol	0 mg

Orange Chocolate Chip Bread

Under 200 Calories

Makes 16 servings

**1 cup skim milk
¼ cup orange juice
⅓ cup sugar
1 egg, slightly beaten
1 tablespoon freshly grated
    orange peel
3 cups all-purpose biscuit
    baking mix
½ cup HERSHEY'S® MINI
    CHIPS Semi-Sweet
    Chocolate**

Heat oven to 350°F. Grease 9×5×3-inch loaf pan. In medium bowl, combine milk, orange juice, sugar, egg and orange peel; stir in baking mix. Beat with spoon until well combined, about 1 minute. Stir in Mini Chips. Pour batter into prepared pan. Bake about 45 to 50 minutes or until wooden pick inserted in center comes out clean. Cool 10 minutes; remove from pan to wire rack. Cool completely. Slice and serve. To store leftovers, wrap in foil or plastic wrap.

Nutrients per serving:

Calories	161	Sodium	274 mg
Fat	5 g	Cholesterol	17 mg

Nutty Blueberry Muffins

Time-Saver Coffeecake

No Cholesterol

Makes 9 servings

Topping

1 cup KELLOGG'S®
COMMON SENSE™ Oat
Bran cereal, any variety
⅓ cup firmly packed brown
sugar
½ teaspoon ground cinnamon
2 tablespoons margarine,
softened

Coffeecake

1½ cups KELLOGG'S®
COMMON SENSE™ Oat
Bran cereal, any variety
1 cup all-purpose flour
½ cup granulated sugar
1 teaspoon baking powder
½ teaspoon ground cinnamon
¼ teaspoon salt
½ cup buttermilk
¼ cup margarine, softened
2 egg whites

1. **For Topping,** combine topping
ingredients in small bowl, mixing until
evenly combined; set aside.

2. **For Coffeecake,** in large mixing
bowl, combine 1½ cups Kellogg's®
Common Sense™ Oat Bran cereal,
flour, granulated sugar, baking
powder, cinnamon and salt. Stir in
buttermilk, ¼ cup margarine and egg
whites, beating until thoroughly
combined. Spread batter evenly in
greased 8-inch square baking pan.
Sprinkle reserved cereal topping over
batter. Cover pan tightly with foil.
Refrigerate overnight or bake
immediately.

3. Bake covered in 350°F oven about
30 minutes or until lightly browned
and wooden pick inserted near center
comes out clean. Cut into squares.
Serve warm.

Nutrients per serving:

Calories	260	Sodium	269 mg
Fat	8 g	Cholesterol	0 mg

Pineapple-Currant Bread

Under 200 Calories

Makes 16 slices

1¾ cups all-purpose flour
½ cup sugar
1½ teaspoons baking powder
¼ teaspoon baking soda
¼ teaspoon salt
3 cups KELLOGG'S® BRAN
FLAKES cereal
1 can (8 ounces) crushed
pineapple, drained
¾ cup orange juice
½ cup currants
¼ cup vegetable oil
3 egg whites

1. Stir together flour, sugar, baking
powder, baking soda and salt; set
aside.

2. In large mixing bowl, beat together
Kellogg's® Bran Flakes cereal and
remaining ingredients until well
mixed. Stir in dry ingredients, mixing
until combined. Spread in lightly
greased 9×5×3-inch loaf pan.

3. Bake in 350°F oven about 55
minutes or until wooden pick inserted
in center comes out clean. Cool 5
minutes before removing from pan.
Let cool completely before slicing.

Nutrients per slice:

Calories	160	Sodium	157 mg
Fat	4 g	Cholesterol	0 mg

Peachy Cinnamon Coffeecake

Low Cholesterol

9 servings

1 can (8¼ ounces) juice pack
    sliced yellow cling peaches
1 package DUNCAN HINES®
    Bakery Style Cinnamon
    Swirl Muffin Mix
1 egg

1. Preheat oven to 400°F. Grease
8-inch square or 9-inch round pan.

2. Drain peaches, reserving juice.
*Add water to reserved juice to equal
¾ cup liquid.* Chop peaches.

3. Combine muffin mix, egg and ¾
cup peach liquid in medium bowl;
fold in peaches. Pour into pan. Knead
swirl packet from Mix 10 seconds
before opening. Squeeze contents on
top of batter and swirl with knife.
Sprinkle contents of topping packet
from Mix over batter. Bake at 400°F
for 28 to 33 minutes for 8-inch pan
(20 to 25 minutes for 9-inch pan) or
until golden. Serve warm.

Nutrients per serving:

Calories	273	Sodium	328 mg
Fat	9 g	Cholesterol	24 mg

Cranberry Oat Bran Muffins

Under 200 Calories

Makes 1 dozen muffins

2 cups flour
1 cup oat bran
½ cup packed brown sugar
2 teaspoons baking powder
½ teaspoon baking soda
½ teaspoon salt (optional)
½ cup MIRACLE WHIP®
    Cholesterol Free Dressing
3 egg whites, slightly beaten
½ cup skim milk
⅓ cup orange juice
1 teaspoon grated orange rind
1 cup coarsely chopped
    cranberries

Preheat oven to 375°. Line 12
medium muffin cups with paper
baking cups or spray with vegetable
cooking spray. Mix together dry
ingredients. Add combined dressing,
egg whites, milk, juice and rind,
mixing just until moistened. Fold in
cranberries. Fill prepared muffin cups
almost full. Bake 15 to 17 minutes or
until golden brown.

Nutrients per muffin:

Calories	190	Sodium	180 mg
Fat	5 g	Cholesterol	0 mg

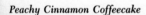

Peachy Cinnamon Coffeecake

Cinnamon Apple-Nut Muffins

Under 200 Calories

Makes 1 dozen muffins

¾ cup peeled, finely chopped apple
½ cup sugar, divided
1 teaspoon ground cinnamon
1 cup all-purpose flour
¾ cup whole wheat flour
2 teaspoons baking powder
¼ teaspoon salt
1 cup low-fat (1%) milk
2 tablespoons margarine, melted
2 egg whites, lightly beaten
¼ cup chopped walnuts
   Sugar, for topping (optional)

Preheat oven to 400°F. In small bowl, toss apple with ¼ cup of the sugar and the cinnamon. In large bowl, combine remaining ¼ cup sugar, the flours, baking powder and salt. Mix together milk, melted margarine and egg whites; stir into dry ingredients just until moistened. Add apple and nuts. Fill lightly greased muffin cups ¾ full; sprinkle each lightly with sugar, if desired. Bake 20 to 25 minutes or until toothpick inserted in center comes out clean.

Nutrients per muffin:

Calories	114	Sodium	177 mg
Fat	4 g	Cholesterol	24 mg

Favorite recipe from **The Sugar Association**

Cocoa Banana-Nut Bread

Low Sodium

Makes 1 loaf, 16 servings

2 extra-ripe, medium DOLE® Bananas, peeled
1½ cups all-purpose flour
1⅓ cups sugar
6 tablespoons unsweetened cocoa
1 teaspoon baking soda
½ teaspoon salt
¼ teaspoon baking powder
2 eggs
½ cup vegetable oil
⅓ cup DOLE® Chopped Almonds

• Place bananas in blender. Process until puréed; use 1 cup for recipe.

• Combine flour, sugar, cocoa, baking soda, salt and baking powder in large bowl. Add eggs, oil and 1 cup banana; beat just until all ingredients are well blended. Stir in almonds.

• Pour batter into greased 9×5-inch loaf pan. Bake in 350°F oven 55 to 60 minutes or until cake tester inserted in center comes out clean. Cool in pan on wire rack 10 minutes. Remove from pan. Cool completely on wire rack before slicing. Loaf may be stored in refrigerator, well wrapped, for 1 week.

Nutrients per serving (1 slice):

Calories	218	Sodium	154 mg
Fat	10 g	Cholesterol	34 mg

Pumpkin-Filled Coffeecake

No Cholesterol

Makes 12 servings

1 cup plus 3 tablespoons sugar, divided
½ cup (1 stick) margarine, softened, divided
3 egg whites
1 teaspoon vanilla
1 cup skim milk
1¾ cups all-purpose flour
1¾ cups QUAKER® Oats (Quick or Old Fashioned, uncooked), divided
1 tablespoon baking powder
1 cup canned pumpkin
½ teaspoon pumpkin pie spice
⅓ cup KRETSCHMER® Original or Honey Crunch Wheat Germ

Heat oven to 350°F. Spray 13×9-inch baking pan with no-stick cooking spray or oil lightly. Beat 1 cup of the sugar and ⅓ cup of the margarine until fluffy. Add egg whites and vanilla; mix well. Stir in milk and combined flour, 1 cup of the oats and the baking powder. Combine 1 cup batter, pumpkin and spice; set aside. Spread half of remaining batter into pan. Top with pumpkin mixture; spread other half of batter over pumpkin. Melt remaining margarine. Combine with remaining ¾ cup oats, 3 tablespoons sugar and the wheat germ. Sprinkle over batter. Bake 30 to 40 minutes or until golden. Refrigerate leftovers.

Nutrients per serving:

Calories	290	Sodium	220 mg
Fat	9 g	Cholesterol	0 mg

Apple Bran Loaf

Apple Bran Loaf

Under 200 Calories

Makes 1 loaf

1½ cups all-purpose flour
½ cup sugar
1 teaspoon baking powder
1 teaspoon baking soda
1 teaspoon ground cinnamon
1½ cups NABISCO® 100% Bran™
1 cup seedless raisins
¼ cup margarine, melted
⅔ cup hot water
1 cup MOTT'S® Regular Apple Sauce
1 egg, slightly beaten
1 teaspoon vanilla extract

In medium bowl, mix flour, sugar, baking powder, baking soda and cinnamon; set aside. In separate bowl, mix bran, raisins, margarine and hot water; let stand 5 minutes. Add apple sauce, egg and vanilla. With mixer at medium speed, beat for 2 minutes. Stir in flour mixture just until blended. Spread in greased 9×5×3-inch loaf pan. Bake at 350°F for 55 minutes or until toothpick inserted in center comes out clean. Cool in pan 10 minutes. Remove from pan; cool on wire rack.

Nutrients per ½-inch-thick slice:

Calories	157	Sodium	161 mg
Fat	4 g	Cholesterol	13 mg

Cottage Cake Muffins

Cottage Cake Muffins

Low Sodium

Makes 20 muffins

2¼ cups all-purpose flour
2 teaspoons baking powder
½ teaspoon baking soda
1 teaspoon ground cinnamon
¼ teaspoon ground nutmeg
¼ teaspoon salt
½ cup butter or margarine, softened
½ cup packed light brown sugar
½ cup granulated sugar
3 eggs
1¾ cups (16-ounce can) LIBBY'S® Solid Pack Pumpkin
¼ cup milk
2 teaspoons orange zest
1 cup chopped assorted dried fruits or raisins
Quick Drizzle Frosting (recipe follows)

In medium mixing bowl, combine flour, baking powder, baking soda, cinnamon, nutmeg, and salt; set aside. In large mixer bowl, cream butter and sugars. Add eggs; beat until light and fluffy. Blend in pumpkin, milk, and orange zest. Add dry ingredients; mix well. Stir in chopped fruits. Spoon mixture into greased muffin cups, filling ¾ full. Bake in preheated 350°F oven for 25 to 30 minutes, or until toothpick inserted in center comes out clean. Immediately remove from pans; cool on wire racks. Drizzle with Quick Drizzle Frosting.

Quick Drizzle Frosting: In small bowl, combine 1 cup sifted powdered sugar and 2 to 3 tablespoons cream or fresh lemon juice.

Nutrients per muffin:			
Calories	196	Sodium	180 mg
Fat	6 g	Cholesterol	46 mg

Lemon Cranberry Loaves

Under 200 Calories

Makes 24 slices

1¼ cups finely chopped fresh
    cranberries
½ cup finely chopped walnuts
¼ cup granulated sugar
1 package DUNCAN HINES®
    Moist Deluxe Lemon
    Supreme Cake Mix
1 package (3 ounces) cream
    cheese, softened
¾ cup milk
4 eggs
    Confectioners sugar

1. Preheat oven to 350°F. Grease and flour two 8½×4½×2½-inch loaf pans.

2. Stir together cranberries, walnuts and granulated sugar in medium bowl; set aside.

3. Combine cake mix, cream cheese and milk in large bowl. Beat at medium speed with electric mixer for 2 minutes. Add eggs, one at a time, beating well after each addition. Fold in cranberry mixture. Pour into pans. Bake at 350°F for 45 to 50 minutes or until toothpick inserted in center comes out clean. Cool in pans 15 minutes. Loosen loaves from pans. Invert onto cooling rack. Turn right-side up. Cool completely. Dust with confectioners sugar.

Nutrients per slice:

Calories	143	Sodium	165 mg
Fat	6 g	Cholesterol	40 mg

Apple Sauce Bran Muffins

Low Cholesterol

Makes 1 dozen muffins

1½ cups NABISCO® 100%
    Bran™
1½ cups MOTT'S® Regular or
    Natural Apple Sauce
1 egg, slightly beaten
¼ cup margarine, melted
½ cup firmly packed light
    brown sugar
1½ cups all-purpose flour
1 tablespoon baking powder
1 teaspoon ground cinnamon
½ cup seedless raisins, optional
    Apple Sauce Glaze (recipe
    follows)

In large bowl, mix bran, apple sauce, egg, margarine and brown sugar; let stand 5 minutes. In separate bowl, blend flour, baking powder and cinnamon; stir in bran mixture just until blended (batter will be lumpy). Stir in raisins if desired. Spoon batter into 12 greased 2½-inch muffin-pan cups. Bake at 400°F for 15 to 18 minutes or until toothpick inserted in center comes out clean. Remove from pan. Cool slightly. Drizzle with Apple Sauce Glaze; serve warm.

Apple Sauce Glaze: Blend ½ cup confectioners' sugar into 1 tablespoon MOTT'S® Regular or Natural Apple Sauce until smooth.

Nutrients per muffin:

Calories	221	Sodium	232 mg
Fat	5 g	Cholesterol	18 mg

Lemon Glazed Peach Muffins

Low Cholesterol

Makes 8 muffins

- 1 cup all-purpose flour
- 3 tablespoons sugar
- 2 teaspoons baking powder
- ½ teaspoon salt
- ½ teaspoon pumpkin pie spice
- 1 can (16 ounces) sliced cling peaches in light syrup
- 1 cup KELLOGG'S® ALL-BRAN® cereal
- ½ cup skim milk
- 1 egg white
- 2 tablespoons vegetable oil
- Lemon Sauce (recipe follows)

1. Stir together flour, sugar, baking powder, salt and pumpkin pie spice. Set aside.

2. Drain peaches reserving ⅓ cup syrup. Set aside 8 peach slices; chop remaining peach slices.

3. Measure Kellogg's® All-Bran® cereal, milk and the ⅓ cup syrup into large mixing bowl. Stir to combine. Let stand 2 minutes or until cereal is softened. Add egg white and oil. Beat well. Stir in chopped peaches.

4. Add flour mixture, stirring only until combined. Portion batter evenly into 8 lightly greased 2½-inch muffin-pan cups. Place 1 peach slice over top of each muffin.

5. Bake at 400°F about 25 minutes or until golden brown. Serve warm with Lemon Sauce.

Lemon Sauce

- ⅓ cup sugar
- 2 tablespoons cornstarch
- 1½ cups cold water
- 1 teaspoon grated lemon peel
- 1 tablespoon lemon juice

Combine sugar and cornstarch in 2-quart saucepan. Add water, stirring until smooth. Cook over medium heat, stirring constantly, until mixture boils. Continue cooking and stirring 3 minutes longer. Remove from heat; stir in lemon peel and juice. Serve hot over warm peach muffins.

Nutrients per serving (1 muffin plus 3 tablespoons sauce):

Calories	210	Sodium	355 mg
Fat	4 g	Cholesterol	1 mg

Carrot Raisin Coffee Cake

Under 200 Calories

Makes 12 servings

- ⅓ cup margarine, melted
- ⅓ cup firmly packed brown sugar
- 2 eggs
- 1 teaspoon vanilla
- 1½ cups QUAKER® Oats (Quick or Old Fashioned, uncooked)
- ¾ cup all-purpose flour
- 1 teaspoon ground cinnamon
- ¾ teaspoon baking powder
- ¼ teaspoon baking soda
- 1 cup shredded carrots
- ⅓ cup raisins
- ¼ cup chopped nuts

Heat oven to 375°F. Lightly spray 8-inch square baking pan with no-stick cooking spray or oil lightly. Combine margarine, sugar, eggs and vanilla; mix well. Add oats, flour, cinnamon, baking powder and baking soda; mix well. Stir in carrots, raisins and nuts. Spread into prepared pan; bake 25 to 30 minutes or until wooden pick inserted in center comes out clean.

Nutrients per serving:

Calories	180	Sodium	120 mg
Fat	8 g	Cholesterol	35 mg

Blueberry Orange Loaf

Blueberry Orange Loaf

No Cholesterol

Makes 12 slices

1 package **DUNCAN HINES®**
  Bakery Style Blueberry
  Muffin Mix
½ teaspoon baking powder
2 egg whites
⅔ cup **CITRUS HILL®** Orange
  Juice
1 teaspoon grated orange peel

1. Preheat oven to 350°F. Grease one 8½×4½×2½-inch or 9×5×3-inch loaf pan.

2. Rinse blueberries from Mix with cold water and drain.

3. Empty muffin mix into bowl. Add baking powder; stir to combine and break up any lumps. Add egg whites and orange juice. Stir until moistened, about 50 strokes. Fold in blueberries and orange peel. Pour into pan. Sprinkle contents of topping packet from Mix over batter. Bake at 350°F for 45 to 55 minutes or until toothpick inserted in center comes out clean. Cool in pan 10 minutes. Loosen loaf from pan. Invert onto cooling rack. Turn right-side up. Cool completely.

Nutrients per slice:			
Calories	189	Sodium	268 mg
Fat	5 g	Cholesterol	0 mg

Cookie

◇◇◇

MAGIC

Cocoa Brownies

No Cholesterol

Makes 18 brownies

   4 **egg whites**
½ cup **CRISCO® PURITAN® Oil**
   1 teaspoon **vanilla extract**
1⅓ cups **sugar**
½ cup **unsweetened cocoa**
1¼ cups **all-purpose flour**
¼ teaspoon **salt**

1. Preheat oven to 350°F. Oil bottom of 9-inch square pan. Set aside.

2. Place egg whites in large bowl. Beat with spoon until slightly frothy. Add Crisco® Puritan® Oil and vanilla. Mix thoroughly. Stir in sugar and cocoa. Mix well. Stir in flour and salt until blended. Pour into pan.

3. Bake at 350°F for 26 to 28 minutes or until brownies start to pull away from side of pan. *Do not overbake.* Cool completely. Cut into bars. Sprinkle with confectioners sugar, if desired.

Nutrients per brownie:

Calories	150	Sodium	43 mg
Fat	7 g	Cholesterol	0 mg

Chocolate Chip Cookies

Under 100 Calories

Makes 3 dozen cookies

   2 cups **all-purpose flour**
   1 teaspoon **baking soda**
½ teaspoon **salt**
   1 **egg**
   3 tablespoons **water**
   1 teaspoon **vanilla extract**
   1 cup **firmly packed brown sugar**
¼ cup **CRISCO® PURITAN® Oil**
½ cup **semi-sweet chocolate chips**

1. Heat oven to 375°F. Oil baking sheets well. Combine flour, baking soda and salt. Set aside. Combine egg, water and vanilla. Set aside.

2. Blend brown sugar and Crisco® Puritan® Oil in large bowl at low speed of electric mixer. Add egg mixture. Beat until smooth. Add flour mixture in three parts at lowest speed. Scrape bowl well after each addition. Stir in chocolate chips.

3. Drop dough by rounded teaspoonfuls onto baking sheets. Bake at 375°F for 7 to 8 minutes or until lightly browned. Cool on baking sheets 1 minute. Remove to cooling racks.

Nutrients per cookie:

Calories	74	Sodium	57 mg
Fat	3 g	Cholesterol	6 mg

Cocoa Brownies (top) and Chocolate Chip Cookies (bottom)

Lemon Cookies

Jelly-Filled Dainties

Under 100 Calories

Makes 4 dozen cookies

2 cups all-purpose flour
½ teaspoon salt
**2¼ cups KELLOGG'S® CORN
    FLAKES cereal**
1 cup margarine, softened
**½ cup firmly packed brown
    sugar**
1 egg
½ teaspoon vanilla extract
**1 cup currant, raspberry or
    strawberry jelly**

1. Stir together flour and salt; set aside. Crush Kellogg's® Corn Flakes cereal into fine crumbs, about ½ cup; set aside.

2. In large bowl, blend margarine and sugar. Add egg and vanilla; beat well. Stir in flour mixture.

3. Shape dough into 1-inch balls. Roll in cereal. Place about 2 inches apart on ungreased baking sheets. Make an indentation in each cookie using handle of wooden spoon.

4. Bake at 300°F for 8 to 10 minutes. Remove from oven; press down indentation in each cookie. Return to oven and bake about 10 minutes longer or until lightly browned. Cool on baking sheets 1 minute. Cool completely on wire racks. When cool, fill centers with about 1 teaspoon jelly.

Nutrients per cookie:

Calories	84	Sodium	82 mg
Fat	4 g	Cholesterol	4 mg

Lemon Cookies

Under 100 Calories

Makes 4 dozen cookies

**⅔ cup MIRACLE WHIP® Salad
    Dressing**
1 two-layer yellow cake mix
2 eggs
2 teaspoons grated lemon peel
**⅔ cup ready-to-spread vanilla
    frosting**
4 teaspoons lemon juice

• Preheat oven to 375°.

• Blend salad dressing, cake mix and eggs at low speed with electric mixer until moistened. Add lemon peel. Beat on medium speed 2 minutes. (Dough will be stiff.)

• Drop rounded teaspoonfuls of dough, 2 inches apart, onto greased cookie sheets.

• Bake 9 to 11 minutes or until lightly browned. (Cookies will still appear soft.) Cool 1 minute; remove from cookie sheets. Cool completely.

• Stir together frosting and juice until well blended. Spread on cookies.

Nutrients per cookie:

Calories	80	Sodium	100 mg
Fat	4 g	Cholesterol	10 mg

Baked Truffle Treasures

Makes 30 cookies

1 cup granulated sugar
¼ cup (½ stick) butter, melted
2 eggs, beaten
3 tablespoons cherry brandy or
    amaretto *or* ½ teaspoon
    almond extract
2 tablespoons honey
1 teaspoon vanilla extract
2 cups ALMOND DELIGHT®
    brand cereal, crushed
    to 1 cup
½ cup unsweetened cocoa
½ cup flaked coconut
½ cup powdered sugar

Preheat oven to 350°. In medium bowl, beat granulated sugar and butter. Add eggs, brandy, honey and vanilla, stirring until well combined. Stir in cereal, cocoa and coconut. Pour into ungreased 2-quart casserole. Bake 30 minutes. Remove from oven and stir immediately until well blended. Let cool to room temperature. Shape level tablespoons of mixture into 1½-inch balls. Roll each ball in powdered sugar. Store in airtight container.

Microwave Directions:
Follow directions above for combining ingredients. Pour batter into ungreased microwave-safe 2-quart casserole dish. Microwave on HIGH 5 to 6 minutes, turning dish ¼ turn halfway through cooking time. Remove from microwave and stir immediately until well blended. Let cool to room temperature. Shape as directed above.

Nutrients per cookie:			
Calories	78	Sodium	39 mg
Fat	3 g	Cholesterol	18 mg

Tropical Bar Cookies

Makes 16 bars

½ cup DOLE® Sliced Almonds,
    divided
1 cup all-purpose flour
⅓ cup margarine, melted
½ cup sugar, divided
1 package (8 ounces) light
    cream cheese, softened
1 egg
1 teaspoon vanilla extract
1 can (20 ounces) DOLE®
    Crushed Pineapple in
    Syrup, drained°
⅓ cup flaked coconut

- Chop ¼ cup almonds for crust; mix with flour, margarine and ¼ cup sugar in medium bowl until crumbly. Press into bottom of 9-inch square pan. Bake in 350°F oven 12 minutes.

- Beat cream cheese, egg, remaining ¼ cup sugar, vanilla and pineapple in large bowl until blended. Pour over crust. Top with coconut and remaining ¼ cup sliced almonds.

- Bake in 350°F oven 35 to 40 minutes until golden brown. Cool on wire rack. Refrigerate at least 2 hours before cutting into bars.

°*Use pineapple packed in juice, if desired.*

Nutrients per cookie:			
Calories	199	Sodium	111 mg
Fat	10 g	Cholesterol	28 mg

Tropical Bar Cookies

Painted Desert Brownies

Makes 40 brownies

3 cups **RICE CHEX®** brand cereal, crushed to 1 cup
1 cup all-purpose flour
¾ cup granulated sugar
½ teaspoon baking powder
½ cup margarine or butter, melted
4 teaspoons instant coffee, dissolved in 2 teaspoons boiling water, divided
1 package (21.5 ounces) chocolate brownie mix
1 package (8 ounces) cream cheese
1 egg, beaten
¼ cup powdered sugar

Preheat oven to 350°. In large bowl combine cereal, flour, granulated sugar and baking powder. Add margarine and 1 teaspoon of the coffee mixture, stirring until well combined. Press evenly and firmly into ungreased 13×9×2-inch baking pan. Bake 10 minutes. Meanwhile prepare brownie mix according to package directions but do not bake; set aside. In medium bowl, beat cream cheese, egg, powdered sugar and remaining 1 teaspoon coffee mixture until well combined. Pour reserved brownie mixture over hot crust. Spoon cream cheese mixture in several places over brownie mixture. Swirl cream cheese mixture into brownie mixture with knife. Bake 30 to 35 minutes or until set. Cool. Cut into squares.

Nutrients per brownie:

Calories	145	Sodium	120 mg
Fat	6 g	Cholesterol	20 mg

Layered Fruit Bars

Makes 20 bars

Base and Topping
⅓ cup **CRISCO®** Shortening
½ cup firmly packed brown sugar
¼ teaspoon vanilla extract
1 cup all-purpose flour
⅛ teaspoon salt (optional)
2 teaspoons skim milk
¼ cup quick oats (not instant or old-fashioned), uncooked

Filling
1 cup apricot preserves

Drizzle
¾ cup confectioners sugar
1 tablespoon plus ½ teaspoon skim milk
¼ teaspoon vanilla extract

1. Preheat oven to 375°F.

2. **For Base**, cream Crisco®, brown sugar and vanilla in large bowl at medium speed of electric mixer. Mix in flour, salt (if used) and milk. Reserve ¼ cup mixture for topping. Press remaining mixture evenly in bottom of ungreased 8-inch square pan. Bake at 375°F for 10 minutes or until lightly browned.

3. **For Topping,** combine reserved ¼ cup mixture with oats until crumbly.

4. **For Filling,** spread preserves over hot baked base. Sprinkle with Topping. Bake at 375°F for 15 minutes or until top is lightly browned. Cool completely.

5. **For Drizzle,** combine confectioners sugar, milk and vanilla. Drizzle over top. Allow to set before cutting into bars.

Nutrients per bar cookie:

Calories	132	Sodium	18 mg
Fat	3 g	Cholesterol	0 mg

Apricot-Pecan Tassies

Apricot-Pecan Tassies

Low Sodium

Makes 24 cookies

- 1 cup all-purpose flour
- ½ cup butter, cut into pieces
- 6 tablespoons light cream cheese
- ¾ cup light brown sugar, firmly packed
- 1 egg, lightly beaten
- 1 tablespoon butter, softened
- ½ teaspoon vanilla extract
- ¼ teaspoon salt
- ⅔ cup Dried California Apricot Halves, diced (about 4 ounces)
- ⅓ cup chopped pecans

In food processor, combine flour, ½ cup butter and cream cheese; process until mixture forms a ball. Wrap dough in plastic wrap and chill 15 minutes. Meanwhile, prepare filling by combining brown sugar, egg, 1 tablespoon butter, vanilla and salt in medium bowl; beat until smooth. Stir in apricots and nuts. Preheat oven to 325°F. Shape dough into 24 (1-inch) balls and place in paper-lined or greased (1½-inch) miniature muffin cups or tart pans. Press dough on bottom and sides of each cup; fill with 1 teaspoon apricot-pecan filling. Bake 25 minutes or until golden and filling sets. Cool slightly and remove from cups. Cookies can be wrapped tightly in plastic and frozen for up to 6 weeks.

Nutrients per cookie:

Calories	110	Sodium	85 mg
Fat	7 g	Cholesterol	13 mg

Favorite recipe from **California Apricot Advisory Board**

Chocolate Chip Raspberry Jumbles

Chocolate Chip Raspberry Jumbles

Low Sodium

Makes 16 bars

**1 package DUNCAN HINES®
  Chocolate Chip Cookie Mix
½ cup seedless red raspberry
  jam**

1. Preheat oven to 350°F.

2. Prepare chocolate chip cookie mix following package directions for original recipe. Reserve ½ cup dough.

3. Spread remaining dough into ungreased 9-inch square pan. Spread jam over base. Drop reserved dough by measuring teaspoonfuls randomly over jam. Bake at 350°F for 20 to 25 minutes or until golden brown. Cool completely. Cut into bars.

Nutrients per cookie:

Calories	178	Sodium	95 mg
Fat	6 g	Cholesterol	13 mg

Spectacular Cannolis

Low Cholesterol

Makes 40 cookies

**1 (8 oz.) container
  PHILADELPHIA BRAND®
  Soft Cream Cheese with
  Strawberries
2 tablespoons milk
2 (5½ oz.) boxes pirouette
  cookies
¾ cup BAKER'S® Real Semi-
  Sweet Chocolate Chips**

• Blend cream cheese and milk in small bowl until smooth.

• Spoon cream cheese mixture into pastry bag; pipe into cookies. Chill 10 minutes.

• Melt chocolate chips in small saucepan over low heat, stirring constantly until smooth. Drizzle cookies with chocolate. Chill.

Nutrients per serving (2 cookies):

Calories	180	Sodium	40 mg
Fat	4 g	Cholesterol	5 mg

Mocha Cookies

Under 100 Calories

Makes 40 cookies

2½ **tablespoons instant coffee**
1½ **tablespoons skim milk**
⅓ **cup light brown sugar**
¼ **cup granulated sugar**
¼ **cup margarine**
1 **egg**
½ **teaspoon almond extract**
2 **cups all-purpose flour, sifted**
¼ **cup wheat flakes cereal**
½ **teaspoon ground cinnamon**
¼ **teaspoon baking powder**

Preheat oven to 350°F. Spray cookie
sheets with non-stick cooking spray.
In small cup, dissolve coffee in milk.
In large bowl, cream together sugars
and margarine. Beat in egg, almond
extract and coffee mixture. Stir
together flour, wheat flakes,
cinnamon and baking powder; beat
into sugar mixture gradually. Drop by
teaspoonfuls, 2 inches apart, onto
cookie sheets. Flatten with back of
fork. Bake 8 to 10 minutes or until
set. Remove from cookie sheets. Cool
completely.

Nutrients per cookie:

Calories	44	Sodium	21 mg
Fat	1 g	Cholesterol	5 mg

Favorite recipe from **The Sugar Association**

Chocolate Candy Cookies

Under 100 Calories

Makes 4½ dozen cookies

⅔ **cup MIRACLE WHIP® Salad
    Dressing**
1 **two-layer devil's food
    cake mix**
2 **eggs**
1 **(8 oz.) pkg. multicolored milk
    chocolate candies**

• Preheat oven to 375°.

• Blend salad dressing, cake mix and
eggs at low speed with electric
mixer until moistened. Beat on
medium speed 2 minutes. Stir in
candies. (Dough will be stiff.)

• Drop rounded teaspoonfuls of
dough, 2 inches apart, onto greased
cookie sheets.

• Bake 9 to 11 minutes or until almost
set. (Cookies will still appear soft.)
Cool 1 minute; remove from cookie
sheets.

Nutrients per cookie:

Calories	80	Sodium	95 mg
Fat	3 g	Cholesterol	10 mg

Cranberry Thumbprints

Low Cholesterol

Makes 2 dozen cookies

1 **cup OCEAN SPRAY® Cran-
    Fruit™ Sauce**
1 **package (20 ounces)
    refrigerated sugar cookie
    dough**
½ **cup powdered sugar**
1 **tablespoon water**

Preheat oven to 350°F. Drain Cran-
Fruit™. Roll dough to form 24
(1-inch) balls. Place on cookie sheets;
press thumb into center of each ball.
Place scant 1 teaspoon Cran-Fruit™
in the indent of each cookie. Bake 7
to 11 minutes or until lightly
browned. Cool slightly before
transferring to wire rack. Combine
powdered sugar and water; drizzle
glaze onto each cookie.

Nutrients per cookie:

Calories	145	Sodium	131 mg
Fat	6 g	Cholesterol	14 mg

Cocoa Banana Bars

No Cholesterol

Makes 9 bars

⅔ cup QUAKER® Oat Bran hot
   cereal, uncooked
⅔ cup all-purpose flour
½ cup granulated sugar
⅓ cup unsweetened cocoa
½ cup mashed ripe banana
   (about 1 large)
¼ cup liquid vegetable oil
   margarine
3 tablespoons light corn syrup
2 egg whites, slightly beaten
1 teaspoon vanilla
2 teaspoons unsweetened cocoa
2 teaspoons liquid vegetable oil
   margarine
¼ cup powdered sugar
2 to 2½ teaspoons warm water,
   divided
   Strawberry halves (optional)

Heat oven to 350°F. Lightly spray
8-inch square baking pan with no-
stick cooking spray or oil lightly.
Combine oat bran, flour, granulated
sugar and ⅓ cup cocoa. Add
combined banana, ¼ cup margarine,
corn syrup, egg whites and vanilla;
mix well. Pour into prepared pan,
spreading evenly. Bake 23 to 25
minutes or until center is set. Cool on
wire rack; cut into bars. Store tightly
covered.

Combine 2 teaspoons cocoa and 2
teaspoons margarine. Stir in
powdered sugar and 1 teaspoon of the
water. Gradually add remaining 1 to
1½ teaspoons water to make
medium-thick glaze; mixing well.
Drizzle glaze over brownies. Top with
strawberry halves, if desired.

Microwave Directions:
Combine oat bran, flour, granulated
sugar and ⅓ cup cocoa. Add
combined banana, ¼ cup margarine,
corn syrup, egg whites and vanilla;
mix well. Pour into 9-inch
microwavable pie plate, spreading

evenly. Place in microwave on
inverted microwavable plate.
Microwave at HIGH 4 minutes 30
seconds to 5 minutes or until edges
are firm to the touch, rotating every 2
minutes. The bars are done when the
surface is firm to the touch; the
center may appear slightly wet and
soft. Cool; cut into wedges. Store
tightly covered. Drizzle with glaze as
directed above.

Nutrients per bar cookie:

Calories	210	Sodium	60 mg
Fat	7 g	Cholesterol	0 mg

Almond Macaroons

Under 100 Calories

Makes 3 dozen cookies

4 egg whites
⅔ cup sugar
One 12-oz. pkg. (2 cups)
      NESTLÉ® TOLL HOUSE®
      Semi-Sweet Chocolate
      Mini Morsels
1½ cups ground blanched
      almonds
½ teaspoon almond extract

Preheat oven to 350°F. Grease cookie
sheets. In large mixer bowl, beat egg
whites until foamy. Gradually add
sugar, beating until stiff peaks form.
Fold in mini morsels, almonds and
almond extract. Drop by heaping
measuring teaspoonfuls onto
prepared cookie sheets.

Bake 20 minutes or until lightly
browned and set. Let stand on cookie
sheets 2 minutes. Remove from
cookie sheets; cool.

Nutrients per cookie:

Calories	97	Sodium	7 mg
Fat	6 g	Cholesterol	0 mg

Cocoa Banana Bars

Banana Cookies

Low Sodium

Makes 4 dozen cookies

2 ripe, medium DOLE®
   Bananas, peeled
1½ cups all-purpose flour
   ½ teaspoon baking soda
   ½ teaspoon salt
   ½ teaspoon ground cinnamon
   ¼ teaspoon ground nutmeg
1½ cups brown sugar, packed
   ¾ cup margarine, softened
   1 egg
   ½ cup light dairy sour cream
   1 teaspoon vanilla extract
1½ cups rolled oats
   1 cup DOLE® Golden Raisins
   ¾ cup DOLE® Chopped
      Almonds, toasted

- Place bananas in blender. Process until puréed; use 1 cup for recipe.

- Combine flour, baking soda, salt and spices in small bowl.

- Beat brown sugar and margarine in large bowl until light and fluffy. Beat in 1 cup bananas, egg, sour cream and vanilla.

- Beat in flour mixture until well blended. Stir in oats, raisins and almonds. Cover and refrigerate dough 1 hour to firm.

- Drop batter by heaping tablespoonfuls onto greased cookie sheets 2 inches apart.

- Bake in 350°F oven 15 to 20 minutes or until cookies are slightly brown around edges. Cool on wire racks.

Nutrients per cookie:

Calories	113	Sodium	72 mg
Fat	5 g	Cholesterol	7 mg

Cranberry-Orange Muesli Bars

No Cholesterol

Makes 24 bars

Filling
   1 package (12 ounces)
      cranberries, fresh or frozen
   1 cup granulated sugar
   1 teaspoon grated orange peel,
      optional
   1 cup orange juice

Base and Topping
   4 cups RALSTON® Brand Fruit
      & Nut Muesli cereal,
      crushed to 3 cups
1½ cups all-purpose flour
   ¾ cup packed brown sugar
1½ teaspoons baking powder
   ½ teaspoon salt
   ¾ cup (1½ sticks) margarine or
      butter, softened

To prepare Filling: In medium saucepan over medium heat combine cranberries, granulated sugar, orange peel and orange juice. Cook, stirring frequently, until mixture comes to a boil; reduce heat and simmer 15 to 18 minutes, stirring frequently. Cool.

To prepare Base and Topping: Preheat oven to 350°. In large bowl combine cereal, flour, brown sugar, baking powder and salt. Mix in margarine until crumbly. Reserve 1½ cups mixture for topping; set aside. Press remaining cereal mixture firmly and evenly into ungreased 13×9×2-inch baking pan. Bake 10 minutes. Spread cranberry filling evenly over base; sprinkle with reserved 1½ cups cereal mixture. Bake an additional 18 to 20 minutes or until lightly browned.

Nutrients per 2-inch bar:

Calories	199	Sodium	167 mg
Fat	7 g	Cholesterol	0 mg

Cholesterol-Free Chocolate Oatmeal Cookies

Low Sodium

Makes 2 dozen cookies

2¼ cups quick oats, uncooked
1 cup all-purpose flour
½ teaspoon baking soda
½ teaspoon cinnamon
¾ cup sugar
½ cup (1 stick) margarine, softened
2 egg whites
1 teaspoon vanilla extract
One 6-oz. pkg. (1 cup) NESTLÉ® TOLL HOUSE® Semi-Sweet Chocolate Morsels

Preheat oven to 350°F. In small bowl, combine oats, flour, baking soda and cinnamon; set aside.

In large mixer bowl, beat sugar, margarine, egg whites and vanilla extract until creamy. Gradually stir in flour mixture and semi-sweet chocolate morsels. Drop by rounded tablespoonfuls onto ungreased cookie sheets.

Bake 12 to 15 minutes. Let stand on cookie sheets 2 minutes. Remove from cookie sheets; cool.

Nutrients per cookie:

Calories	144	Sodium	66 mg
Fat	6 g	Cholesterol	0 mg

Peanut Butter Bars

Under 100 Calories

Makes 24 bars

1 package DUNCAN HINES® Peanut Butter Cookie Mix
2 egg whites
½ cup chopped peanuts
1 cup confectioners sugar
2 tablespoons water
½ teaspoon vanilla extract

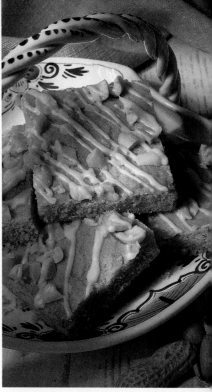

Peanut Butter Bars

1. Preheat oven to 350°F.

2. Combine cookie mix, contents of peanut butter packet from Mix and egg whites in large bowl. Stir until thoroughly blended. Press in ungreased 13×9×2-inch pan. Sprinkle peanuts over dough. Press lightly. Bake at 350°F for 16 to 18 minutes or until golden brown. Cool completely.

3. Combine confectioners sugar, water and vanilla extract in small bowl. Stir until blended. Drizzle glaze over top. Cut into bars.

Nutrients per cookie:

Calories	65	Sodium	104 mg
Fat	7 g	Cholesterol	0 mg

Raisin, Oat & Almond Bars

No Cholesterol

Makes 20 bars

- **2 cups QUAKER® Oats (Quick or Old Fashioned, uncooked)**
- **1½ cups all-purpose flour**
- **¾ cup firmly packed brown sugar**
- **½ teaspoon baking soda**
- **¼ teaspoon grated lemon peel**
- **¼ teaspoon ground cinnamon**
- **¾ cup (1½ sticks) margarine, melted**
- **1½ cups raisins**
- **⅔ cup water**
- **2 tablespoons granulated sugar**
- **2 teaspoons cornstarch**
- **⅓ cup sliced almonds**

Heat oven to 350°F. Lightly spray 13×9-inch baking pan with no-stick cooking spray or oil lightly. Combine oats, flour, brown sugar, baking soda, lemon peel and cinnamon. Add margarine, mixing until crumbly. Reserve 1 cup for topping; press remaining mixture onto bottom of prepared pan. Bake 15 minutes.

In small saucepan, combine remaining ingredients except almonds and reserved 1 cup oat topping; bring to a boil, stirring frequently. Reduce heat; simmer 30 seconds to 1 minute or until thickened and clear, stirring constantly. Cool slightly. Pour over crust. Sprinkle with reserved topping and almonds. Bake 20 to 25 minutes or until edges are lightly browned. Cool; cut into bars. Store loosely covered in cool place.

Microwave Directions:
Prepare crust and topping as directed above. For raisin filling, combine raisins, water, granulated sugar and cornstarch in 1-qt. microwavable measuring cup or bowl. Microwave at HIGH 2 minutes; stir. Microwave an additional 1 minute 30 seconds to 2 minutes or until thickened and clear, stirring every minute. Cool slightly. Proceed as above.

Nutrients per bar cookie:

Calories	210	Sodium	110 mg
Fat	8 g	Cholesterol	0 mg

Peanut Butter Cookies

Under 100 Calories

Makes 4 dozen cookies

- **⅔ cup firmly packed light brown sugar**
- **½ cup chunky or smooth peanut butter**
- **⅓ cup BLUE BONNET® Margarine, softened**
- **1 egg**
- **½ cup Regular, Instant or Quick CREAM OF WHEAT® Cereal, uncooked**
- **1 teaspoon vanilla extract**
- **1¼ cups all-purpose flour**
- **½ teaspoon baking soda**

In medium bowl, with electric mixer at medium speed, beat brown sugar, peanut butter, margarine and egg until fluffy; blend in cereal and vanilla. Stir in flour and baking soda to make a stiff dough. Roll dough into 1-inch balls; place 2 inches apart on greased baking sheets. Flatten balls with bottom of floured glass; press with fork tines to make crisscross pattern. Bake at 350°F for 8 to 9 minutes or until lightly browned. Remove from baking sheets; cool on wire racks.

Nutrients per cookie:

Calories	59	Sodium°	34 mg
Fat	3 g	Cholesterol	4 mg

°If Using Quick CREAM OF WHEAT®, sodium is 40 mg.

Chocolate Biscotti

Under 100 Calories

Makes 4 dozen cookies

1½ cups all-purpose flour
½ cup NESTLÉ® Cocoa
1½ teaspoons baking powder
½ teaspoon baking soda
⅔ cup sugar
3 tablespoons butter, softened
2 eggs
½ teaspoon almond extract
½ cup almonds, coarsely
    chopped

Preheat oven to 350°F. Grease
15½×10½×1-inch baking pan. In
small bowl, combine flour, cocoa,
baking powder and baking soda; set
aside.

In large mixer bowl, beat sugar,
butter, eggs and almond extract until
creamy. Gradually beat in flour
mixture. Stir in almonds. Divide
dough in half. Shape into two 12-inch
long logs; flatten slightly. Place in
prepared pan.

Bake 25 minutes. Cool in pan on wire
rack 5 minutes. Cut into ½-inch thick
slices; return slices to pan, cut-sides
down. Bake 20 minutes longer. Cool
completely.

Nutrients per cookie:

Calories	46	Sodium	29 mg
Fat	2 g	Cholesterol	11 mg

Orange Sugar Cookies

No Cholesterol

Makes 3½ dozen cookies

2 cups all-purpose flour
1½ teaspoons baking soda
1 cup sugar
½ cup FLEISCHMANN'S®
    Margarine, softened
2 teaspoons grated orange peel
1 teaspoon vanilla extract
¼ cup EGG BEATERS® 99%
    Real Egg Product
    Sugar, optional

In small bowl, combine flour and
baking soda; set aside.

In medium bowl, with electric mixer
at medium speed, beat sugar,
margarine, orange peel and vanilla
until creamy. Add Egg Beaters®; beat
1 minute. Gradually stir in flour
mixture until blended. Chill dough 1
hour.

Shape dough into 42 (¾-inch) balls;
roll in sugar if desired. Place 2 inches
apart on lightly greased baking sheets.
Bake at 375°F for 8 to 10 minutes or
until light golden brown. Remove
from baking sheets. Cool on wire
racks.

Nutrients per cookie:

Calories	60	Sodium	49 mg
Fat	2 g	Cholesterol	0 mg

Chocolate Biscotti

Cool

◇◇◇

DELIGHTS

Bavarian Rice Cloud with Bittersweet Chocolate Sauce

Under 200 Calories

Makes 10 servings

1 envelope unflavored gelatin
1½ cups skim milk
3 tablespoons sugar
2 cups cooked rice
2 cups frozen light whipped topping, thawed
1 tablespoon almond-flavored liqueur
½ teaspoon vanilla extract
  Vegetable cooking spray
  Bittersweet Chocolate Sauce (recipe follows)
2 tablespoons sliced almonds, toasted

Sprinkle gelatin over milk in small saucepan; let stand 1 minute or until gelatin is softened. Cook over low heat, stirring constantly, until gelatin dissolves. Add sugar and stir until dissolved. Add rice; stir until well blended. Cover and chill until the consistency of unbeaten egg whites. Fold in whipped topping, liqueur, and vanilla. Spoon into 4-cup mold coated with cooking spray. Cover and chill until firm. To serve, unmold onto serving platter. Spoon chocolate sauce over rice dessert. Sprinkle with toasted almonds.

Bittersweet Chocolate Sauce

3 tablespoons unsweetened cocoa
3 tablespoons sugar
½ cup low-fat buttermilk
1 tablespoon almond-flavored liqueur

Combine cocoa and sugar in small saucepan. Add buttermilk, mixing well. Place over medium heat, and cook until sugar dissolves. Stir in liqueur; remove from heat.

Tip: Unmold gelatin desserts onto slightly dampened plate. This will allow you to move the mold and position it where you want it on the plate.

Nutrients per serving:

Calories	146	Sodium	211 mg
Fat	3 g	Cholesterol	1 mg

Favorite recipe from **USA Rice Council**

*Bavarian Rice Cloud with
Bittersweet Chocolate Sauce*

From left to right: Cranberry Apple Ice, Orange Apple Ice and Apple Honeydew Ice

Cranberry Apple Ice

Under 100 Calories

Makes 14 (½-cup) servings

**1 (12-ounce) can frozen apple-
cranberry juice
concentrate, thawed
1½ cups MOTT'S® Chunky Apple
Sauce
1 (32-ounce) bottle (4 cups)
sugar-free lemon-lime
flavored carbonated
beverage**

In 2-quart non-metal bowl, combine
all ingredients; mix well. Cover;
freeze until firm. Scoop frozen
mixture into 5-ounce drink cups or
into dessert dishes.

Nutrients per serving:

Calories	33	Sodium	14 mg
Fat	0 g	Cholesterol	0 mg

Orange Apple Ice

Under 100 Calories

Makes 12 (½-cup) servings

**1 (23-ounce) jar MOTT'S®
Natural or Regular Apple
Sauce
⅓ cup orange marmalade
3 egg whites, beaten stiff°**

In medium bowl, combine apple
sauce and marmalade; mix well.
Carefully fold in beaten egg whites.
Pour into 8- or 9-inch square pan.
Cover; freeze until firm. Scoop frozen
mixture into 5-ounce cups, dessert
dishes or orange shells (see Tip).
Garnish as desired.

*Tip: To make shell or cup, use a sharp
knife to make sawtooth-cut around
middle of fruit, cutting inside to
center only. Twist, pull apart and
remove inside portion, scraping shells
clean with spoon.*

°Use only clean, uncracked eggs.

Nutrients per serving:

Calories	51	Sodium	15 mg
Fat	0 g	Cholesterol	0 mg

Apple Honeydew Ice

Makes 10 (½-cup) servings

- **2 cups sugar-free lemon-lime flavored carbonated beverage**
- **1 cup MOTT'S® Regular Apple Sauce**
- **1 small honeydew melon, seeded, rind removed, cut into chunks**
- **⅛ teaspoon ground ginger**
- **2 to 3 drops green food color, if desired**

In food processor or blender, combine all ingredients; process until smooth. Pour into 8- or 9-inch non-metal square pan. Cover; freeze until firm. Scoop frozen mixture into 5-ounce cups or into dessert dishes. Garnish as desired.

Nutrients per serving:

Calories	37	Sodium	14 mg
Fat	0 g	Cholesterol	0 mg

Cranberry Sorbet

Makes 6 servings

- **1 package OCEAN SPRAY® Cran-Fruit™ Sauce**
- **2 cups OCEAN SPRAY® Cranberry Juice Cocktail**
- **1 cup corn syrup**

In large bowl, combine all ingredients. Pour into 13×9-inch pan and freeze until firm. Cut mixture into small pieces. Process in food processor until smooth and light. Pour back into pan and refreeze until firm.

Nutrients per serving:

Calories	300	Sodium	36 mg
Fat	0 g	Cholesterol	0 mg

Peach Melba Parfaits

Makes 6 parfaits

- **1 (10-ounce) package frozen red raspberries in syrup, thawed**
- **¼ cup red currant jelly**
- **1 tablespoon cornstarch**
- **½ (½-gallon carton) BORDEN® or MEADOW GOLD® Peach Frozen Yogurt**
- **⅔ cup granola or natural cereal**

Drain raspberries, reserving ⅔ cup syrup. In small saucepan, combine reserved syrup, jelly and cornstarch. Cook and stir until slightly thickened and glossy. Cool. Stir in raspberries. In parfait or wine glasses, layer raspberry sauce, frozen yogurt, raspberry sauce then granola; repeat. Freeze. Remove from freezer 5 to 10 minutes before serving. Garnish as desired. Freeze leftovers.

Nutrients per serving:

Calories	268	Sodium	75 mg
Fat	5 g	Cholesterol	9 mg

Peach Melba Parfait

Chilled Lemonade Dessert

Makes 8 servings

1½ cups cold water
1 (3 oz.) pkg. JELL-O® Brand Lemon Flavor Sugar Free Gelatin Dessert
1 (8 oz.) pkg. PHILADELPHIA BRAND® LIGHT Neufchatel Cheese, softened
⅓ cup frozen lemonade concentrate, thawed
1 teaspoon grated lemon peel
2 cups COOL WHIP® Non-Dairy Whipped Topping, thawed

• Bring water to boil. Gradually add to gelatin in small bowl; stir until dissolved.

• Beat neufchatel cheese, lemonade concentrate and peel in large mixing bowl at medium speed with electric mixer until well blended. Stir in gelatin; chill until thickened but not set.

• Fold in whipped topping; pour into lightly oiled 6-cup mold. Chill until firm. Unmold. Garnish with peach slices, blueberries and fresh mint leaves, if desired.

Variation: Substitute eight individual ½-cup molds for 6-cup mold.

Nutrients per serving:			
Calories	160	Sodium	150 mg
Fat	10 g	Cholesterol	25 mg

Chilled Lemonade Dessert

Pumpkin Pie Ice Cream

Makes 1½ quarts

3 cups (two 12-ounce cans) *undiluted* CARNATION® Evaporated Milk
1¾ cups (16-ounce can) LIBBY'S® Solid Pack Pumpkin
1½ cups granulated sugar
½ teaspoon pumpkin pie spice
⅛ teaspoon salt

In blender container, place evaporated milk, pumpkin, sugar, pumpkin pie spice, and salt; blend on low speed. Pour into ice cream maker and freeze according to manufacturer's instructions.

Variation: For fruit or berry ice cream, combine in large bowl, 2 cups fruit pulp,° 3 cups evaporated milk, 1½ cups sugar, 2 teaspoons lemon juice, and ⅛ teaspoon salt. Freeze as above. *Makes about 2 quarts.*

°*Any fruit or berries may be used. If using sweetened frozen fruit, reduce sugar to ½ cup.*

Nutrients per ½ cup serving:			
Calories	195	Sodium	90 mg
Fat	5 g	Cholesterol	19 mg

Jell-O® Sugar Free Jigglers

Jell-O® Sugar Free Jigglers

Under 100 Calories

Makes 8 dozen cubes

2½ cups boiling water
4 packages (4-serving size each)
or 2 packages (8-serving
size each) JELL-O® Brand
Sugar Free Gelatin, any
flavor

ADD boiling water to gelatin.
Dissolve completely. Pour into 13×9-
inch pan. Chill until firm, about 3
hours.

DIP pan in warm water about 15
seconds for easy removal. Cut gelatin
into 1-inch squares. (Or use cookie
cutters to cut decorative shapes; cut
remaining gelatin into cubes.)

Notes: For thicker Jell-O® Sugar Free
Jigglers, use 8- or 9-inch square pan.

To use ice cube trays or Jell-O®
Jiggler molds, pour gelatin mixture
into 2 or 3 ice cube trays. Chill until
firm, about 2 hours. To remove, dip
trays in warm water about 15
seconds. Moisten tips of fingers and
gently pull from edges.

Nutrients per cube:

Calories	2	Sodium	10 mg
Fat	0 g	Cholesterol	0 mg

Mocha-Spice Dessert (top) and Chocolate Mousse (bottom)

Chocolate Mousse

Under 100 Calories

Makes 2⅔ cups or 5 servings

1½ cups cold skim milk
1 package (4-serving size)
    JELL-O® Chocolate Flavor
    Sugar Free Instant Pudding
    and Pie Filling
1 cup thawed COOL WHIP
    LITE™ Whipped Topping
¼ cup fresh raspberries

• Pour milk into medium mixing
  bowl. Add pudding mix. Beat with
  wire whisk until well blended, 1 to 2
  minutes. Gently stir in whipped
  topping. Spoon into individual
  dishes or medium serving bowl.
  Refrigerate until ready to serve. Top
  with raspberries. Garnish if desired.

Nutrients per serving:			
Calories	90	Sodium	310 mg
Fat	2 g	Cholesterol	0 mg

Mocha-Spice Dessert

No Cholesterol

Makes 6 servings

2 cups cold skim milk
1 package (4-serving size)
   JELL-O® Chocolate Flavor
   Sugar Free Instant Pudding
   and Pie Filling
1 tablespoon MAXWELL
   HOUSE® or YUBAN®
   Instant Coffee or SANKA®
   Brand 99.7% Caffeine Free
   Instant Coffee
1½ cups thawed COOL WHIP
   LITE™ Whipped Topping
¼ teaspoon ground cinnamon

• Pour milk into large mixing bowl. Add pudding mix and instant coffee. Beat with wire whisk until well blended, 1 to 2 minutes. Pour into medium serving bowl or individual dishes. Refrigerate.

• Just before serving, combine whipped topping and cinnamon; spread over pudding. Garnish if desired.

Nutrients per serving:

Calories	90	Sodium	270 mg
Fat	3 g	Cholesterol	0 mg

Strawberry Ice

Under 200 Calories

Makes 6 servings

1 quart fresh strawberries,
   cleaned and hulled (about
   1½ pounds)
1 cup sugar
½ cup water
3 tablespoons REALEMON®
   Lemon Juice from
   Concentrate
   Red food coloring, optional

In blender container, combine sugar, water and ReaLemon® brand; mix well. Gradually add strawberries; blend until smooth, adding food coloring if desired. Pour into 8-inch square pan; freeze about 1½ hours. In small mixer bowl, beat until slushy. Return to freezer in square pan. Place in refrigerator 1 hour before serving to soften. Freeze leftovers.

Nutrients per serving:

Calories	162	Sodium	3 mg
Fat	0 g	Cholesterol	0 mg

Peach Ice Cream

Under 100 Calories

Makes 7 cups

7 fresh California peaches
1 envelope unflavored gelatin
2 cups low-fat milk
1 cup plain low-fat yogurt
½ cup sugar
1 tablespoon vanilla extract

Chop enough peaches to measure 1 cup. Purée remaining peaches in blender or food processor to measure 2½ cups. Sprinkle gelatin over milk in medium saucepan. Let stand 1 minute to soften. Stir over medium heat until gelatin dissolves; remove from heat. Add chopped peaches, peach purée, yogurt, sugar and vanilla extract to gelatin mixture; mix well. Prepare in ice cream maker according to manufacturer's instructions. Pack into containers. Freeze until firm.

Nutrients per ½ cup serving:

Calories	85	Sodium	30 mg
Fat	1 g	Cholesterol	4 mg

Favorite recipe from **California Tree Fruit Agreement**

Frozen Apple Sauce 'n Fruit Cup

Makes 7 (½-cup) servings

1 cup MOTT'S® Chunky or
   Regular Apple Sauce
1 (10-ounce) package frozen
   strawberries, thawed
1 (11-ounce) can mandarin
   orange segments, drained
1 cup grapes
2 tablespoons orange juice
   concentrate

In medium bowl, combine all
ingredients. Spoon fruit mixture into
individual dishes or paper cups.
Freeze until firm. Remove from
freezer about 30 minutes before
serving.

Nutrients per serving:

Calories	107	Sodium	5 mg
Fat	0 g	Cholesterol	0 mg

Frozen Apple Sauce 'n Fruit Cup

Apricot Mousse

Makes 6 servings

1 (32-ounce) container
   DANNON® Vanilla Lowfat
   Yogurt
2 cans (16 ounces *each*) apricot
   halves in heavy syrup,
   drained
1 tablespoon sugar
1½ teaspoons orange-flavored
   liqueur (optional)
1 cup fresh blueberries, rinsed
   and drained
4 fresh strawberries, hulled and
   thinly sliced
   Mint sprigs for garnish
   (optional)

Line large strainer with double
thickness of cheesecloth or triple
layer of paper towels. Place strainer
over large bowl to catch the liquid
(whey) that will drain off. Spoon
yogurt into strainer. Cover and
refrigerate overnight. Scrape drained
yogurt into medium bowl. Discard the
whey. Process apricots to a smooth
purée in food processor or blender.
Add to yogurt with sugar and liqueur;
stir to mix well. Cover and chill at
least 30 minutes. To serve, divide
blueberries among 6 wine glasses or
dessert dishes, reserving a few berries
for the top. Spoon mousse over
berries. Arrange a few strawberry
slices over each glass. Sprinkle with
remaining blueberries and garnish
with mint.

Nutrients per serving:

Calories	200	Sodium	100 mg
Fat	3 g	Cholesterol	5 mg

Lite Chocolate Mint Parfaits

Under 200 Calories

Makes 7 servings

⅔ cup sugar
¼ cup HERSHEY'S® Cocoa
3 tablespoons cornstarch
Dash salt
2½ cups cold skim milk, divided
1 tablespoon margarine
1½ teaspoons vanilla extract, divided
1 envelope whipped topping mix (to make 2 cups whipped topping)
¼ teaspoon mint extract
3 to 4 drops green food color (optional)

In medium saucepan, combine sugar, cocoa, cornstarch and salt; gradually stir in 2 cups of the milk. Cook over medium heat, stirring constantly, until mixture boils; boil and stir 1 minute. Remove from heat; blend in margarine and 1 teaspoon of the vanilla. Pour into medium bowl. Press plastic wrap directly onto surface of pudding; refrigerate. In small bowl, combine topping mix, remaining ½ cup milk and ½ teaspoon vanilla; prepare according to package directions. Fold ½ cup of the topping into pudding. Blend mint extract and green food color into remaining topping. Alternately spoon chocolate pudding and mint whipped topping into parfait glasses. Refrigerate until thoroughly chilled.

Nutrients per serving:

Calories	175	Sodium	104 mg
Fat	4 g	Cholesterol	2 mg

Sparkling Lemon Ice

Sparkling Lemon Ice

Under 100 Calories

Makes 6 servings

1 package (4-serving size) JELL-O® Brand Lemon Flavor Sugar Free Gelatin
1 cup boiling water
1 cup cold lemon-lime seltzer
3 tablespoons fresh lemon juice
½ teaspoon grated lemon peel

• Completely dissolve gelatin in boiling water. Add seltzer, lemon juice and peel. Pour into 8- or 9-inch square pan; cover. Freeze until firm, about 3 hours.

• Remove from freezer; let stand at room temperature 10 minutes to soften slightly. Beat at medium speed with electric mixer or process with food processor until smooth. Spoon or scoop into individual dishes. Serve immediately.

Nutrients per serving:

Calories	8	Sodium	50 mg
Fat	0 mg	Cholesterol	0 mg

Cocoa Chiffon Dessert

Under 100 Calories

Makes 8 servings

1 envelope unflavored gelatin
3 tablespoons sugar
3 tablespoons HERSHEY'S®
　　Cocoa
1¾ cups skim milk
½ teaspoon vanilla extract
1 envelope dry whipped
　　topping mix (to make
　　2 cups whipped topping)
½ cup cold skim milk

In medium saucepan, mix gelatin with sugar; add cocoa. Blend in 1¾ cups milk; let stand 5 minutes. Stir over low heat with wire whisk until gelatin is completely dissolved, about 5 minutes. Remove from heat; stir in vanilla. Refrigerate until mixture begins to thicken. In medium bowl, combine topping mix and ½ cup cold milk; prepare according to package directions. Fold 1½ cups whipped topping into cocoa mixture. Spoon into dessert dishes. Cover; refrigerate until firm. Garnish with remaining topping.

Variation: 1 teaspoon brandy extract may be substituted for vanilla.

Nutrients per serving:			
Calories	78	Sodium	35 mg
Fat	2 g	Cholesterol	1 mg

Lemon Banana Yogurt Pops

Under 200 Calories

Makes 6 servings

2 egg whites°
2 tablespoons sugar
1 ripe banana
2 cartons (8 ounces each) low-
　　fat lemon-flavored yogurt

In small bowl, beat egg whites until soft peaks form. Gradually add sugar, beating until stiff peaks form. In blender or food processor, combine banana and yogurt; process until smooth. In large bowl, fold egg white mixture into yogurt mixture. Divide mixture among 6 popsicle molds or 5-ounce paper cups. Insert wooden popsicle sticks. Freeze until solid. Remove from molds or peel away paper cups.

°*Use only clean, uncracked eggs.*

Nutrients per serving:			
Calories	120	Sodium	61 mg
Fat	1 g	Cholesterol	3 mg

Favorite recipe from The Sugar Association

Strawberry Yogurt Angel

Low Cholesterol

Makes 12 servings

1 (8 oz.) container
　　PHILADELPHIA BRAND®
　　Soft Cream Cheese with
　　Strawberries
½ cup vanilla yogurt
½ cup orange juice
1 tablespoon orange flavored
　　liqueur (optional)
1 10-inch tube angel food cake,
　　sliced
1 pt. strawberries, sliced

• Place cream cheese, yogurt, orange juice and liqueur in food processor or blender container; process until smooth.

• Serve cream cheese sauce over cake slices; top with strawberries.

Nutrients per serving:			
Calories	220	Sodium	130 mg
Fat	6 g	Cholesterol	15 mg

Tiramisu

Makes 12 servings

1½ cups cold 2% lowfat milk,
    divided
1 container (8 ounces)
    pasteurized process cream
    cheese product
2 tablespoons MAXWELL
    HOUSE® or YUBAN®
    Instant Coffee or SANKA®
    Brand 99.7% Caffeine Free
    Instant Coffee
1 tablespoon water
2 tablespoons brandy (optional)
1 package (4-serving size)
    JELL-O® Vanilla Flavor
    Sugar Free Instant Pudding
    and Pie Filling
2 cups thawed COOL WHIP
    LITE™ Whipped Topping
1 package (3 ounces)
    ladyfingers, split
1 square (1 ounce) BAKER'S®
    Semi-Sweet Chocolate,
    grated

- Pour ½ cup of the milk into blender container. Add cream cheese product; cover. Blend until smooth. Blend in the remaining 1 cup milk.

- Dissolve coffee in water; add to blender with brandy. Add pudding mix; cover. Blend until smooth, scraping down sides occasionally; pour into large mixing bowl. Gently stir in whipped topping.

- Cut ladyfingers in half crosswise. Cover bottom of 8-inch springform pan with ladyfinger halves. Place remaining halves, cut-ends down, around sides of pan. Spoon pudding mixture into pan. Chill until firm, about 3 hours. Remove side of pan. Sprinkle with grated chocolate.

Nutrients per serving:

Calories	140	Sodium	240 mg
Fat	6 g	Cholesterol	35 mg

Tiramisu

Melon Bubbles

Makes 7 (½-cup) servings

1 package (4-serving size)
    JELL-O® Brand Sugar Free
    Gelatin, any flavor
¾ cup boiling water
½ cup cold water
    Ice cubes
1 cup melon balls (cantaloupe,
    honeydew or watermelon)
    Mint leaves (optional)

DISSOLVE gelatin in boiling water.
Combine cold water and ice cubes to
make 1¼ cups. Add to gelatin,
stirring until slightly thickened.
Remove any unmelted ice. Measure
1⅓ cups gelatin into small bowl; add
melon. Pour into dessert dishes or
serving bowl.

WHIP remaining gelatin at high
speed of electric mixer until fluffy,
thick and about doubled in volume.
Spoon over gelatin in glasses. Chill
until set, about 2 hours. Garnish with
additional melon balls and mint
leaves, if desired.

Nutrients per serving:

Calories	14	Sodium	50 mg
Fat	0 g	Cholesterol	0 mg

Fresh Peach Sorbet

Makes about 1 quart

7 fresh California peaches,
    quartered
¾ cup sugar
3 tablespoons light corn syrup
1 teaspoon lemon juice

Purée peaches in blender or food
processor to measure 3½ cups.
Combine peach purée, sugar, corn
syrup and lemon juice in saucepan.
Cook over low heat until sugar
dissolves. Cool to room temperature.
Prepare in ice cream maker according
to manufacturer's instructions. Pack
into containers. Freeze until firm.

Nutrients per ¼ cup serving:

Calories	69	Sodium	3 mg
Fat	0 g	Cholesterol	0 mg

Favorite recipe from California Tree Fruit
Agreement

Lemon Rice Dessert

Makes 8 servings

1 package (3 ounces) lemon-
    flavored gelatin dessert
1 cup boiling water
½ cup cold water
1 cup cooked rice, chilled
1½ cups frozen whipped topping,
    thawed
¼ cup sliced almonds
¼ cup chopped maraschino
    cherries
1 tablespoon grated lemon peel

Dissolve gelatin in boiling water; add
cold water. Place bowl in ice water
and stir until gelatin is the consistency
of unbeaten egg whites; stir in rice.
Fold in whipped topping until
smooth. Lightly fold in almonds,
cherries, and lemon peel. Continue to
stir gently (over ice) until thickened.
Pour into dessert dishes. Cover and
chill until ready to serve.

Nutrients per serving:

Calories	131	Sodium	149 mg
Fat	3 g	Cholesterol	2 mg

Favorite recipe from USA Rice Council

Melon Bubbles

Ambrosia Fruit Custard

Under 200 Calories

Makes 4 servings

1 package (4-serving size)
   sugar-free instant vanilla
   pudding
   Ingredients for pudding
1 teaspoon DOLE® Lemon zest
1 tablespoon DOLE® Lemon
   juice
½ teaspoon coconut or almond
   extract
1 can (8 ounces) DOLE®
   Pineapple Tidbits in juice,
   drained
1 cup assorted sliced DOLE®
   fresh fruit
¼ cup mini marshmallows or
   flaked coconut

- Make pudding according to package directions in bowl. Stir in lemon zest, lemon juice and coconut extract. Reserve ¼ cup pudding for topping.

- Spoon remaining pudding equally into dessert bowls. Combine remaining ingredients in bowl except reserved pudding. Spoon on top of pudding. Top with reserved pudding.

Nutrients per serving:

Calories	139	Sodium	203 mg
Fat	2 g	Cholesterol	0 mg

Grape Yogurt Pops

Under 200 Calories

Makes 8 servings

2 cups (1 pint) plain lowfat
   yogurt
1 can (6 ounces) frozen orange
   juice concentrate, thawed
⅓ cup sugar
2 cups California seedless
   grapes

Combine yogurt, orange juice concentrate and sugar in large bowl; stir until concentrate is smooth and sugar dissolves. Pour into 8 (4-ounce) waxed paper cups. Drop ¼ cup grapes into each cup. Freeze until almost firm. Insert wooden ice cream stick in center of each cup. Freeze until firm. To serve, peel off cup.

Note: For longer storage, wrap pops in plastic wrap to prevent dehydration.

Nutrients per serving:

Calories	146	Sodium	42 mg
Fat	1 g	Cholesterol	3 mg

Favorite recipe from **California Table Grape Commission**

Orange Lemon Sorbet

No Cholesterol

Makes 6 servings

1 cup sugar
1 cup water
1½ cups orange juice
⅓ cup REALEMON® Lemon
   Juice from Concentrate
1 teaspoon grated orange rind
2 tablespoons orange-flavored
   liqueur, optional

In medium saucepan, combine sugar and water. Over medium heat, bring to a boil; boil 5 minutes. Remove from heat; chill 20 minutes. Add remaining ingredients to sugar syrup. Pour into 8- or 9-inch square pan; freeze about 1½ hours or until slightly frozen. In large mixer bowl, beat until smooth; return to pan. Cover. Freeze at least 1½ hours before serving. If storing longer, remove from freezer 5 minutes before serving. Return leftovers to freezer.

Nutrients per serving:

Calories	159	Sodium	4 mg
Fat	0 g	Cholesterol	0 mg

Rice Pudding

Rice Pudding

Low Cholesterol

Makes 6 servings

- 3 cups 2% low-fat milk
- 1 large stick cinnamon
- 1 cup uncooked long-grain white rice
- 2 cups water
- ½ teaspoon salt
  Peel of an orange or lemon
- ¾ cup sugar
- ¼ cup raisins
- 2 tablespoons dark rum

Heat milk and cinnamon in small saucepan over medium heat until milk is infused with flavor of cinnamon, about 15 minutes. Combine rice, water, and salt in 2- to 3-quart saucepan. Bring to a boil; stir once or twice. Place orange peel on top of rice. Reduce heat, cover, and simmer 15 minutes or until rice is tender and liquid is absorbed. Remove and discard orange peel. Strain milk and stir into cooked rice. Add sugar and simmer 20 minutes or until thickened, stirring often. Add raisins and rum; simmer 10 minutes. Serve cold or hot. To reheat, add a little milk to restore creamy texture.

Tip: Use medium or short grain rice for rice pudding with a creamier consistency.

Nutrients per serving:

Calories	297	Sodium	259 mg
Fat	3 g	Cholesterol	10 mg

Favorite recipe from **USA Rice Council**

Nectarine Raspberry Ice

Makes about 2 quarts

- 1 envelope unflavored gelatin
- ½ cup cold water
- ½ cup dry white wine
- ⅓ cup sugar
- 1 package (10 ounces) unsweetened frozen raspberries, thawed
- 4 fresh California nectarines, cut into chunks
- 1 teaspoon lemon zest
- ¼ cup lemon juice

Sprinkle gelatin over water in saucepan. Let stand 1 minute to soften. Stir over medium heat until gelatin dissolves. Stir in wine and sugar; cook and stir until sugar is dissolved. Remove from heat; set aside. Purée raspberries, nectarines, lemon zest and lemon juice in blender. Combine with wine syrup. Turn into shallow pan and freeze until firm. Soften slightly, then beat smooth with mixer. Refreeze and keep frozen until ready to serve. Garnish with nectarine slices, if desired.

Nutrients per ½ cup serving:			
Calories	62	Sodium	1 mg
Fat	0 g	Cholesterol	0 mg

Favorite recipe from **California Tree Fruit Agreement**

Nectarine Raspberry Ice

Raspberry Rice aux Amandes

Makes 8 servings

- 3 cups cooked rice
- 2 cups skim milk
- ⅛ teaspoon salt
  Low-calorie sugar substitute to equal 2 tablespoons sugar
- 1 teaspoon vanilla extract
- ¾ cup frozen light whipped topping, thawed
- 3 tablespoons sliced almonds, toasted
- 1 package (16 ounces) frozen unsweetened raspberries, thawed°

Combine rice, milk, and salt in 2-quart saucepan. Cook over medium heat until thick and creamy, 5 to 8 minutes, stirring frequently. Remove from heat. Cool. Add sugar substitute and vanilla. Fold in whipped topping and almonds. Alternate rice mixture and raspberries in parfait glasses or dessert dishes.

Microwave Directions:
Combine rice, milk, and salt in 1½-quart microproof baking dish. Cover and cook on HIGH 3 minutes. Reduce setting to MEDIUM (50% power) and cook 7 minutes, stirring after 3 and 5 minutes. Stir in sugar substitute and vanilla; cool. Fold in whipped topping and almonds. Alternate rice mixture and raspberries in parfait glasses or dessert dishes.

°Substitute frozen unsweetened strawberries or other fruit for the raspberries, if desired.

Nutrients per serving:			
Calories	180	Sodium	369 mg
Fat	3 g	Cholesterol	2 mg

Favorite recipe from **USA Rice Council**

Frozen Banana Dessert Cups

No Cholesterol

Makes 8 to 12 servings

2 extra-ripe, medium DOLE®
   Bananas, peeled
1 cup DOLE® Fresh or frozen
   Strawberries
1 can (8 ounces) DOLE®
   Crushed Pineapple in
   Juice, drained
2 tablespoons honey
   Dash ground nutmeg
1 cup frozen whipped topping,
   thawed
¼ cup DOLE® Chopped
   Almonds
1 cup DOLE® Pure & Light
   Mountain Cherry Juice
1 tablespoon cornstarch
1 tablespoon sugar
   Sliced DOLE® fresh fruit, for
   garnish

Frozen Banana Dessert Cup

- Place bananas, strawberries, pineapple, honey and nutmeg in blender. Process until smooth. Fold in whipped topping and almonds.

- Line 12 muffin cups with foil liners. Fill with banana mixture. Cover and freeze until firm.

- Blend cherry juice, cornstarch and sugar in small saucepan. Cook, stirring, until sauce boils and thickens. Cool.

- To serve, spoon cherry sauce onto each serving plate. Remove foil liners from dessert. Invert on top of sauce. Arrange fresh fruit around mold.

Nutrients per serving:

Calories	99	Sodium	4 mg
Fat	3 g	Cholesterol	0 mg

Creamy Frozen Yogurt

Under 100 Calories

Makes 7 (½-cup) servings

1 package (4-serving size)
   JELL-O® Brand Sugar Free
   Gelatin, any flavor
1 cup boiling water
½ cup cold water
1 container (8 ounces) plain
   lowfat yogurt
2 cups thawed COOL WHIP®
   Whipped Topping

DISSOLVE gelatin in boiling water. Add cold water. Stir in yogurt until well blended and smooth. Fold in whipped topping. Pour into 9-inch square pan. Freeze until firm, about 6 hours or overnight. Scoop into individual dessert dishes.

Nutrients per serving:

Calories	80	Sodium	60 mg
Fat	4 g	Cholesterol	5 mg

Fruitful

◇◇◇

PLEASURES

Strawberries Elegante

Under 200 Calories

Makes 6 servings

6 cups strawberry slices
2 tablespoons orange flavored
    liqueur or orange juice
1 (8 oz.) container
    PHILADELPHIA BRAND®
    LIGHT Pasteurized Process
    Cream Cheese Product
3 tablespoons brown sugar
1 tablespoon orange flavored
    liqueur or orange juice
1 tablespoon skim milk

• Toss strawberries with 2 tablespoons
liqueur in small bowl.

• Place cream cheese product, sugar,
1 tablespoon liqueur and milk in
food processor or blender container;
process until well blended. Serve
over strawberries. Garnish with
fresh mint leaves, if desired.

Nutrients per serving:

Calories	170	Sodium	220 mg
Fat	7 g	Cholesterol	20 mg

Strawberries Elegante and
Spectacular Cannolis (page 46)

Fruit Trifle

No Cholesterol

Makes 10 servings

1 (10-inch) angel food cake
1 DOLE® Fresh Pineapple
3 firm, medium DOLE®
    Bananas, peeled, divided
3 cups assorted DOLE® fresh
    fruit
1 pint DOLE® Strawberry or
    Raspberry Sorbet
2 DOLE® Kiwifruit, peeled,
    sliced for garnish
1 pint DOLE® Fresh
    Raspberries for garnish
1 cup DOLE® Pine-Orange-
    Guava Juice

• Cut cake in half. Freeze one-half
for another use. Tear remaining
cake into chunks.

• Twist crown from pineapple. Cut in
half lengthwise. Cut fruit from shell
with a knife. Trim off core and cut
fruit into chunks.

• Combine pineapple, 2 of the
bananas, sliced, and 3 cups assorted
fruit in large bowl.

• In 3-quart glass bowl, layer half of
the mixed fruit, cake and sorbet.
Repeat layers. Top with kiwifruit,
raspberries and remaining banana,
sliced. Pour juice over all. Cover
and refrigerate 1 hour or overnight.

Nutrients per serving:

Calories	240	Sodium	54 mg
Fat	1 g	Cholesterol	0 mg

Blueberry Crisp

Blueberry Crisp

No Cholesterol

Makes 8 servings

- **3 cups cooked brown rice**
- **3 cups fresh blueberries°**
- **¼ cup plus 3 tablespoons firmly packed brown sugar, divided**
- **Vegetable cooking spray**
- **⅓ cup rice bran**
- **¼ cup whole-wheat flour**
- **¼ cup chopped walnuts**
- **1 teaspoon ground cinnamon**
- **3 tablespoons margarine**

Combine rice, blueberries, and 3 tablespoons brown sugar. Coat 8 individual custard cups or 2-quart baking dish with cooking spray. Place rice mixture in cups or baking dish; set aside. Combine bran, flour, walnuts, remaining ¼ cup sugar, and cinnamon in bowl. Cut in margarine with pastry blender until mixture resembles coarse meal. Sprinkle over rice mixture. Bake at 375°F. for 15 to 20 minutes or until thoroughly heated. Serve warm.

Microwave Directions:
Prepare as directed using 2-quart microproof baking dish. Cook, uncovered, on HIGH 4 to 5 minutes, rotating dish once during cooking time. Let stand 5 minutes. Serve warm.

°Substitute frozen unsweetened blueberries for the fresh blueberries, if desired. Thaw and drain before using. Or, substitute your choice of fresh fruit or combinations of fruit for the blueberries, if desired.

Nutrients per serving:

Calories	243	Sodium	61 mg
Fat	8 g	Cholesterol	0 mg

Favorite recipe from **USA Rice Council**

Apricot Crumble

Makes 12 servings

- 1 cup dried apricots
- 1¼ cups water
- 2 tablespoons brown sugar (optional)
- 1½ cups all-purpose flour
- ½ cup firmly packed brown sugar
- ¼ teaspoon salt (optional)
- ¼ teaspoon ground cinnamon
- ⅓ cup margarine
- 1 cup KELLOGG'S® ALL-BRAN® cereal
- 3 tablespoons water

1. In 2-quart saucepan, simmer apricots in 1¼ cups water, uncovered, about 20 minutes or until tender. Purée apricots, cooking liquid and 2 tablespoons brown sugar in blender or food processor; set aside.

2. While apricots are simmering, in large mixing bowl, combine flour, ½ cup brown sugar, salt and cinnamon. Using pastry blender, cut in margarine until mixture resembles coarse crumbs. Stir in Kellogg's® All-Bran® cereal; mix well. Add the 3 tablespoons water (mixture will be crumbly). Set aside 1 cup cereal mixture. With back of spoon, press remaining cereal mixture firmly into bottom of ungreased 9-inch square baking pan. Spread puréed apricots evenly over cereal mixture in pan. Sprinkle with reserved cereal mixture, pressing slightly.

3. Bake in 350°F oven about 35 minutes or until lightly browned. Cool completely. Cut into squares to serve.

Nutrients per serving:

Calories	190	Sodium	188 mg
Fat	5 g	Cholesterol	0 mg

Melon Cooler Salad

Makes 8 servings

- 1 (8 oz.) pkg. PHILADELPHIA BRAND® LIGHT Neufchatel Cheese, softened
- ½ cup frozen lemonade or limeade concentrate, thawed
- 4 cups assorted melon balls

- Place neufchatel cheese and lemonade concentrate in food processor or blender container; process until well blended.

- Spoon melon balls into parfait glasses or individual bowls; top with cream cheese mixture.

Nutrients per serving:

Calories	140	Sodium	125 mg
Fat	7 g	Cholesterol	25 mg

Melon Cooler Salad

Fruit Sparkles

Under 100 Calories

Makes 6 (½-cup) servings

1 package (4-serving size)
   JELL-O® Brand Sugar Free
   Gelatin, any flavor
1 cup boiling water
1 cup cold fruit flavor seltzer,
   sparkling water, club soda
   or other sugar free
   carbonated beverage
1 cup sliced banana and
   strawberries°
Mint leaves

DISSOLVE gelatin in boiling water.
Add beverage. Chill until slightly
thickened. Add fruit. Pour into
individual dessert dishes. Chill until
firm, about 1 hour. Garnish with
additional fruit and mint leaves, if
desired.

°*You may substitute 1 cup drained
mandarin orange sections or crushed
pineapple for bananas and
strawberries.*

Nutrients per serving:

Calories	25	Sodium	50 mg
Fat	0 g	Cholesterol	0 mg

5-Minute Apple Crisp

Low Sodium

Makes 6 servings

1 (23-ounce) jar MOTT'S®
   Chunky Apple Sauce
¼ cup margarine
¼ cup firmly packed brown
   sugar
¼ cup fine dry bread crumbs
¼ cup NABISCO® 100% Bran™
¼ cup chopped walnuts
¼ teaspoon ground cinnamon

Divide apple sauce among 6 greased
6-ounce ovenproof dishes. In medium
bowl, blend remaining ingredients
and spoon over apple sauce. Broil 4
inches from heat source 5 minutes or
until top is golden brown.

Nutrients per serving:

Calories	241	Sodium	124 mg
Fat	10 g	Cholesterol	0 mg

Microwave Streusel Pears

No Cholesterol

Makes 6 servings

6 cups sliced, firm fresh pears
   (about 6 medium)
3 tablespoons granulated sugar
1 tablespoon fresh lemon juice
1 cup quick-cooking oats
⅓ cup firmly packed brown
   sugar
2 tablespoons flour
½ teaspoon ground cinnamon
¼ teaspoon ground nutmeg
¼ cup margarine

In large bowl, toss pears with
granulated sugar and lemon juice.
Spray 8-inch square microwave-safe
baking dish lightly with non-stick
cooking spray. Place pears in
prepared dish. Combine oats, brown
sugar, flour and spices. Cut in
margarine using pastry blender or
2 knives until mixture is crumbly.
Sprinkle over pears. Cook uncovered
on HIGH power 7 to 9 minutes or
until pears are tender. Serve warm.

Nutrients per serving:

Calories	295	Sodium	236 mg
Fat	9 g	Cholesterol	0 mg

Favorite recipe from **The Sugar Association**

Fruit Sparkles

Apple Cinnamon Dessert

Under 200 Calories

Makes 2 servings

- 1 cup pared diced apple
- 2 teaspoons REALEMON® Lemon Juice from Concentrate
- 1½ tablespoons sugar
- ⅛ teaspoon ground cinnamon
- 2 slices BORDEN® Lite-line® American Flavor Cheese Product,° cut into small pieces
- ½ tablespoon low-calorie margarine
- 2 plain melba rounds, crushed

Preheat oven to 350°. In small bowl, combine apples, ReaLemon® brand, sugar and cinnamon; mix well. Stir in cheese product. Divide mixture between 2 small baking dishes. Top with margarine; sprinkle with melba crumbs. Bake 12 to 15 minutes or until apples are tender. Refrigerate leftovers.

°*"½ the calories" - 8% milkfat version*

Nutrients per serving:

Calories	123	Sodium	315 mg
Fat	4 g	Cholesterol	5 mg

Apple Cinnamon Dessert

Sautéed Bananas

No Cholesterol

Makes 4 servings

- 2 tablespoons CRISCO® Shortening
- 2 tablespoons orange juice
- 4 firm, ripe bananas
- 2 tablespoons confectioners' sugar

1. Melt Crisco® in large heavy skillet over medium heat. Stir in orange juice.

2. Peel bananas. Cut in half crosswise, then cut each in half lengthwise. Place in skillet and cook over medium heat for 5 minutes, turning once.

3. Arrange bananas in serving dish. Sprinkle with confectioners' sugar. Serve hot.

Nutrients per serving:

Calories	174	Sodium	1 mg
Fat	6 g	Cholesterol	0 mg

Spirited Fruit

Under 100 Calories

Makes about 3 cups

- ¼ cup orange-flavored liqueur *or* orange juice
- 3 tablespoons REALEMON® Lemon Juice from Concentrate
- 2 tablespoons sugar
- 3 cups assorted cut-up fresh fruit

In medium bowl, combine liqueur, ReaLemon® brand and sugar; stir until sugar dissolves. Stir in fruit. Cover; refrigerate 4 hours or overnight, stirring occasionally. Serve with cheesecake, pound cake, ice cream or sherbet. Refrigerate leftovers.

Nutrients per ¼ cup serving:

Calories	47	Sodium	1 mg
Fat	0 g	Cholesterol	0 mg

Nectarine Crème Fraîche

Under 100 Calories

Makes 4 servings

2 fresh California nectarines, sliced
1 cup plain low-fat yogurt
1 teaspoon honey or sugar
Few drops almond extract
1 envelope unflavored gelatin
2 tablespoons cold water

Purée nectarines, yogurt, honey and almond extract in blender. Sprinkle gelatin over water in small saucepan. Let stand 1 minute to soften. Stir over low heat until dissolved. Add to nectarine mixture in blender. Blend 10 seconds. Chill until mixture begins to thicken. Spoon into stemmed glasses and chill until set. Garnish with additional nectarine slices and mint sprigs, if desired.

Nutrients per serving:

Calories	79	Sodium	42 mg
Fat	1 g	Cholesterol	3 mg

Favorite recipe from **California Tree Fruit Agreement**

Grilled Bosc Pears with Walnuts in Apricot Yogurt Sauce

Under 200 Calories

Makes 6 servings

1 orange
1½ cups apricot nectar, divided
½ cup California Walnuts
1½ teaspoons honey
¾ cup plain non-fat yogurt
3 USA ripe Bosc Pears
1 tablespoon California Walnuts, finely chopped

Grilled Bosc Pear with Walnuts in Apricot Yogurt Sauce

Remove orange peel using vegetable peeler. Cut peel into thin strips 1½ inches in length. Place peel and ½ cup of the apricot nectar in small saucepan over medium-low heat and simmer, stirring often, until nectar has evaporated. Set aside.

In food processor or blender, purée ½ cup walnuts with honey and 2 tablespoons of orange juice squeezed from the peeled orange. Set aside.

In mixing bowl, combine yogurt with remaining 1 cup apricot nectar. Halve and core pears. Leaving skins on, cut pears into thin slices so that slices remain attached to stem end. Fan out pear halves and brush lightly with yogurt mixture. Place pear fans, core-side down, in non-stick skillet. Sear pears over high heat until edges are slightly charred. Set aside.

Place ¼ cup apricot-yogurt mixture evenly onto center of each of 6 serving plates. Spoon 1 tablespoon orange-walnut mixture on one side. Arrange pears on top of walnut mixture. Sprinkle with finely chopped walnuts and reserved orange peel. Garnish with red leaf lettuce, if desired.

Nutrients per serving:

Calories	181	Sodium	26 mg
Fat	7 g	Cholesterol	1 mg

Favorite recipe from **Walnut Marketing Board**

Rice Crepes

Makes 10 crepes

1 carton (8 ounces) egg
  substitute°
⅔ cup evaporated skim milk
1 tablespoon margarine,
  melted
½ cup all-purpose flour
1 tablespoon sugar
1 cup cooked rice
  Vegetable cooking spray
2½ cups fresh fruit (strawberries,
  raspberries, blueberries, or
  other favorite fruit)
  Low-sugar fruit spread
  (optional)
  Light sour cream (optional)
1 tablespoon confectioner's
  sugar

Combine egg substitute, milk, and margarine in small bowl. Stir in flour and sugar until smooth and well blended. Stir in rice; let stand 5 minutes. Heat 8-inch nonstick skillet or crepe pan; coat with cooking spray. Spoon ¼ cup batter into pan. Lift pan off heat; quickly tilt pan in rotating motion so that bottom of pan is completely covered with batter. Place pan back on heat and continue cooking until surface is dry, about 45 seconds. Turn crepe over and cook 15 to 20 seconds; set aside. Continue with remaining crepe batter. Place waxed paper between crepes. Spread each crepe with your favorite filling: strawberries, raspberries, blueberries, fruit spread, or sour cream. Roll up and sprinkle with confectioner's sugar for garnish.

°*Substitute 8 egg whites or 4 eggs for 1 carton (8 ounces) egg substitute, if desired.*

Nutrients per crepe:

Calories	111	Sodium	152 mg
Fat	2 g	Cholesterol	1 mg

Favorite recipe from **USA Rice Council**

Grape Angel Dessert

Makes 12 servings

¼ cup orange-flavored liqueur
1 tablespoon corn syrup
1 teaspoon grated orange peel
2 cups California seedless
  grapes
  Orange Custard Sauce
  (recipe follows)
1 prepared angel food cake
  (10 ounces), sliced

Bring liqueur and corn syrup to boil in saucepan; add orange peel. Remove from heat; add grapes and marinate 1 hour. To serve, spoon 2½ tablespoons Orange Custard Sauce over each slice of cake and top with marinated grapes.

Orange Custard Sauce: Cream ¼ cup softened butter or margarine and 1¼ cups powdered sugar in saucepan; add 2 tablespoons orange-flavored liqueur and 2 well-beaten egg yolks.° Stir in ¼ cup half-and-half; cook over low heat until thickened. Beat 2 egg whites until soft peaks form; beat in egg yolk mixture. Serve warm or chilled. Cover and refrigerate until ready to serve.

°*Use only clean, uncracked eggs.*

Nutrients per serving:

Calories	276	Sodium	130 mg
Fat	6 g	Cholesterol	57 mg

Favorite recipe from **California Table Grape Commission**

Rice Crepe

Meringue Fruit Cup with Custard Sauce

Meringue Fruit Cups with Custard Sauce

Low Sodium

Makes 8 servings

4 large egg whites, at room
    temperature
½ teaspoon cream of tartar
    Pinch salt
1 cup sugar
1 can (17 ounces)
    DEL MONTE® Fruit
    Cocktail, drained
    Custard Sauce (recipe
    follows)

Line baking sheet with parchment or waxed paper. With bottom of glass, trace eight 3-inch circles about 2 inches apart on paper. Turn paper over on baking sheet. Beat egg whites until frothy; add cream of tartar and salt. Beat until soft peaks form. Add sugar, 1 tablespoon at a time, and beat until meringue is stiff and shiny, about 10 minutes. Transfer to pastry bag fitted with star tip. Use a little meringue to secure paper to baking sheet. Pipe 2 tablespoons meringue in center of each circle; spread to edges. Pipe 2 rings, one on top of the other, around edges of circles. Bake in preheated 200°F oven about 1½ hours or until dry but still white. Cool completely. (Can be made several days ahead and stored in airtight container.)

Spoon fruit into meringue cups. Place on individual dessert dishes. Spoon approximately ¼ cup Custard Sauce over each. Garnish with mint, if desired.

Custard Sauce

4 egg yolks,° slightly beaten
¼ cup sugar
    Pinch salt
2 cups milk, scalded
1 teaspoon vanilla extract

In top of double boiler, mix egg yolks, sugar and salt until well blended. Slowly add milk, stirring constantly. Cook over hot water, stirring constantly, until mixture begins to thicken. Remove from heat; stir in vanilla. Chill. *Makes about 2½ cups.*

°*Use only clean, uncracked eggs.*

Nutrients per serving:			
Calories	217	Sodium	63 mg
Fat	5 g	Cholesterol	115 mg

Apple Baked Pudding

Under 200 Calories

Makes 8 servings

- 1 cup KELLOGG'S® COMMON SENSE™ Oat Bran cereal, any variety
- ½ cup sugar
- ½ cup all-purpose flour
- 1 tablespoon baking powder
- 1 teaspoon apple pie spice
- 2 cups shredded, cored red cooking apples, about 2 medium
- 3 egg whites
- 1 teaspoon vanilla
- ¼ cup sliced almonds

1. Lightly coat 9-inch glass pie plate with vegetable spray; set aside.

2. In large mixing bowl, combine Kellogg's® Common Sense™ Oat Bran cereal, sugar, flour, baking powder and spice. Add apples, stirring to coat.

3. Stir egg whites and vanilla into cereal mixture, mixing until evenly combined. Spread mixture evenly in prepared pie plate. Sprinkle with almonds.

4. Bake in 325°F oven about 30 minutes or until lightly browned. Serve warm.

Microwave Directions:

Prepare as above. Cook on HIGH 4 minutes or until top is no longer wet and loses shiny appearance. Let stand 5 minutes before serving.

Nutrients per serving:

Calories	150	Sodium	147 mg
Fat	2 g	Cholesterol	0 mg

Fresh Fruit Parfait

Under 100 Calories

Makes 6 (½-cup) servings

- ½ cup blueberries
- ½ cup sliced strawberries
- 1 package (4-serving size) JELL-O® Brand Sugar Free Gelatin, any flavor
- ¾ cup boiling water
- ½ cup cold water
  Ice cubes
- ¾ cup thawed COOL WHIP® Whipped Topping
  Mint leaves (optional)

DIVIDE fruit among 6 parfait glasses. Dissolve gelatin in boiling water. Combine cold water and ice cubes to make 1¼ cups. Add to gelatin, stirring until slightly thickened. Remove any unmelted ice. Measure ¾ cup gelatin; pour over fruit in glasses. Chill until set but not firm.

FOLD whipped topping into remaining gelatin. Spoon into glasses. Chill until set, about 1 hour. Garnish with additional fruit and mint leaves, if desired.

Nutrients per serving:

Calories	40	Sodium	35 mg
Fat	2 g	Cholesterol	0 mg

Fresh Fruit Parfait

Exciting

◇◆◇◆◇

EXTRAS

Lemon Ginger Sauce

No Cholesterol

Makes ½ cup

½ cup **MIRACLE WHIP® FREE Nonfat Dressing**
2 tablespoons lemon juice
1½ tablespoons packed brown sugar
1 teaspoon *each* grated lemon peel, ground ginger

• Mix together ingredients until well blended; refrigerate. Serve over fresh fruit.

Nutrients per serving (2 tablespoons):

Calories	60	Sodium	370 mg
Fat	1 g	Cholesterol	0 mg

Banana Pineapple Colada

No Cholesterol

Makes 2 servings

½ ripe banana
½ cup fresh or canned pineapple
½ cup pineapple juice
½ cup ice cubes
1 tablespoon sugar
¼ teaspoon coconut extract

Combine all ingredients in blender or food processor; process until smooth. Pour and serve immediately.

Nutrients per serving:

Calories	198	Sodium	5 mg
Fat	0 g	Cholesterol	0 mg

Favorite recipe from The Sugar Association

Fruited Yogurt Shake

Under 100 Calories

Makes 9 (½-cup) servings

3 cups cold lowfat milk
1 package (4-serving size) **JELL-O® Sugar Free Instant Pudding and Pie Filling,** any flavor
1 container (8 ounces) plain lowfat yogurt
1 cup crushed ice
1 medium banana, cut into chunks°

COMBINE all ingredients in blender in order given; cover. Blend at high speed 1 minute. Pour into glasses. Serve immediately.

°You may substitute ½ cup sliced strawberries for banana chunks.

Nutrients per serving:

Calories	90	Sodium	210 mg
Fat	2 g	Cholesterol	10 mg

Lemon Ginger Sauce

Quick and Creamy Cocoa Dip for Fruit

Quick and Creamy Cocoa Dip for Fruit

Under 200 Calories

Makes 4 servings

1 carton (8 ounces) low-fat vanilla or honey yogurt
1 tablespoon unsweetened cocoa powder
4 fresh California peaches, plums, nectarines or Bartlett pears (or any combination), sliced

Combine yogurt and cocoa in serving bowl. Serve with sliced fruit.

Tip: To keep fruit colors bright and prevent browning, dip sliced fruit in mixture of 1 tablespoon lemon juice and 1 cup water.

Nutrients per serving:

Calories	116	Sodium	38 mg
Fat	2 g	Cholesterol	0 mg

Favorite recipe from **California Tree Fruit Agreement**

Cranberry Cool

Under 200 Calories

Makes 4 servings

2 cups low calorie cranberry apple drink
½ cup PHILADELPHIA BRAND® LIGHT Pasteurized Process Cream Cheese Product
1 cup frozen vanilla lowfat yogurt

• Gradually add cranberry apple drink to cream cheese product in food processor or blender container; process until blended.

• Add frozen yogurt; process until well blended. Serve over ice, if desired.

Nutrients per serving:

Calories	150	Sodium ·	170 mg
Fat	5 g	Cholesterol	15 mg

Peach Fizz

Makes 6 servings

3 fresh California peaches,
    sliced
1 can (6 ounces) pineapple
    juice
¼ cup frozen limeade or
    lemonade concentrate,
    undiluted
¼ teaspoon almond extract
    Finely crushed ice
3 cups club soda, chilled

Purée peaches in blender or food
processor to measure 2 cups purée.
Stir in pineapple juice, limeade
concentrate and almond extract. Fill
six 12-ounce glasses ⅔ full with
crushed ice. Add ½ cup peach
mixture to each; top with club soda.
Stir gently.

Nutrients per serving:

Calories	65	Sodium	6 mg
Fat	0 g	Cholesterol	0 mg

Favorite recipe from **California Tree Fruit
Agreement**

Iced French Roast

Makes 2 servings

2 cups brewed French roast
    coffee, strong
2 tablespoons low-fat milk
2 teaspoons sugar
½ teaspoon cocoa powder
    Dash ground cinnamon

Combine all ingredients in blender;
blend until smooth. Pour over ice and
serve immediately, or refrigerate to
serve later.

Nutrients per serving:

Calories	27	Sodium	13 mg
Fat	0 g	Cholesterol	1 mg

Favorite recipe from **The Sugar Association**

Cocoa Cinnamon Topper

Makes 1¼ cups

1 cup QUAKER® Oat Bran hot
    cereal, uncooked
1 teaspoon grated orange peel
    (optional)
¼ cup sugar
1 tablespoon unsweetened
    cocoa
½ teaspoon ground cinnamon

Heat oven to 350°F. Place oat bran in
ungreased 13×9-inch baking pan.
Bake 15 to 17 minutes or until light
golden brown, stirring occasionally.
Stir in orange peel; cool. Add sugar,
cocoa and cinnamon. Store tightly
covered at room temperature. To
serve, sprinkle generously on fruit,
fruit salads, low fat yogurt, ice milk or
pudding. Or use as a topping for
muffins by sprinkling on batter just
before baking.

Microwave Directions:
Place oat bran in 1-qt. microwavable
bowl. Microwave at HIGH 2 to 3
minutes, stirring every minute. Stir in
orange peel; cool. Proceed as above.

Nutrients per serving (1 tablespoon):

Calories	25	Sodium	0 mg
Fat	0 g	Cholesterol	0 mg

Cocoa Cinnamon Topper

Apricot Frappé

Low Cholesterol

Makes 6 servings

2 cups apricot nectar
½ cup PHILADELPHIA
    BRAND® LIGHT
    Pasteurized Process Cream
    Cheese Product
1 cup diet ginger ale
3 tablespoons orange juice or
    orange flavored liqueur
½ teaspoon vanilla
3 ice cubes

- Gradually add nectar to cream
  cheese product in food processor or
  blender container; process until
  blended.

- Add ginger ale, orange juice and
  vanilla; process until well blended.
  Add ice; process 1 minute. Serve in
  chilled glasses. Garnish with fresh
  fruit, if desired.

Nutrients per serving:

Calories	100	Sodium	120 mg
Fat	3 g	Cholesterol	10 mg

Strawberry Frosty

Under 200 Calories

Makes 6 servings

1 (8 oz.) container
    PHILADELPHIA BRAND®
    Soft Cream Cheese with
    Strawberries
1 pt. strawberries, hulled
1 cup frozen strawberry lowfat
    yogurt
1 cup diet lemon-lime
    carbonated beverage
1 tablespoon sugar or 3 packets
    sugar substitute

- Place cream cheese and
  strawberries in food processor or
  blender container; process until
  blended.

- Add frozen yogurt, carbonated
  beverage and sugar; process until
  well blended. Serve over ice, if
  desired.

Nutrients per serving:

Calories	190	Sodium	115 mg
Fat	10 g	Cholesterol	35 mg

Apple Butter

Under 100 Calories

Makes about 1 pint (32 servings)

1 pound cooking apples
½ cup water
½ cup packed brown sugar
¼ teaspoon ground cinnamon
    Dash *each* ground cloves and
    allspice

Wash, remove stems and quarter
apples. Place apples and water in
large saucepan and cook slowly until
soft. Squeeze fruit through a fine
strainer to yield 1 cup apple pulp.
Add brown sugar, cinnamon, cloves
and allspice. Cook over low heat,
stirring frequently, until sugar is
dissolved. Continue cooking and
stirring until mixture is thick and
brown and no liquid separates around
edge of butter when a small amount
is spooned onto a saucer.

*Note: For larger amounts (more than
1 pound of apples), measure apple
pulp and add ½ cup packed brown
sugar for each cup of apple pulp.*

Nutrients per 1 tablespoon serving:

Calories	21	Sodium	1 mg
Fat	0 g	Cholesterol	0 mg

Favorite recipe from The Sugar Association

*Apricot Frappé (left) and
Strawberry Frosty (right)*

Banana-Date Shake

Banana-Date Shake

No Cholesterol

Makes 2 servings

**2 ripe, medium DOLE®
   Bananas, peeled
1 DOLE® Orange, peeled
1½ cups DOLE® Pure & Light
   Orchard Peach Juice,
   chilled
¼ cup DOLE® Dates
   Cracked ice, optional**

Place all ingredients in blender except cracked ice. Process until smooth. Add cracked ice while blending for frosty cold shake.

Nutrients per serving:

Calories	205	Sodium	14 mg
Fat	1 g	Cholesterol	0 mg

Fruit Spreads

Under 200 Calories

Makes about 2 cups (10 servings)

**2 cups fresh berries
1½ cups sugar**

Wash, drain and crush berries. In medium saucepan, combine berries and sugar. Cook over medium heat until sugar is dissolved, stirring constantly. Increase heat and bring to a rapid boil, again stirring constantly. Cook about 10 minutes or until jam is thick and small amount dropped onto a saucer stays in place. Cool completely. Fruit spreads should be stored in tightly sealed container in refrigerator and will keep about 4 weeks.

Note: Recipe can be made with blackberries, blueberries, raspberries or strawberries.

Nutrients per serving:

Calories	117	Sodium	1 mg
Fat	0 g	Cholesterol	0 mg

Favorite recipe from **The Sugar Association**

Pear Berry Crush

Under 100 Calories

Makes 2 servings

**1 package (10 ounces)
   unsweetened frozen
   raspberries or strawberries
1 fresh California Bartlett pear,
   cored, coarsely chopped
12 ice cubes, cracked**

Combine all ingredients in blender; blend until smooth.

Nutrients per serving:

Calories	97	Sodium	3 mg
Fat	0 g	Cholesterol	0 mg

Favorite recipe from **California Tree Fruit Agreement**

Acknowledgments

The publishers would like to thank the companies and organizations listed below for the use of their recipes in this publication.

Best Foods, a Division of CPC International Inc.
Borden Kitchens, Borden, Inc.
California Apricot Advisory Board
California Table Grape Commission
California Tree Fruit Agreement
Carnation, Nestlé Food Company
Checkerboard Kitchens, Ralston Purina Company
Chilean Winter Fruit Association
The Dannon Company, Inc.
Del Monte Corporation
Dole Food Company, Inc.
Hershey Chocolate U.S.A.
Keebler Company
Kellogg Company

Kraft General Foods, Inc.
Libby's, Nestlé Food Company
Mott's U.S.A., A division of Cadbury Beverages Inc.
Nabisco Foods Group
Nestlé Chocolate and Confection Company
New York Cherry Growers Association, Inc.
Ocean Spray Cranberries, Inc.
The Procter & Gamble Company, Inc.
The Quaker Oats Company
The Sugar Association, Inc.
USA Rice Council
Walnut Marketing Board

Photo Credits

The publishers would like to thank the companies and organizations listed below for the use of their photographs in this publication.

Best Foods, a Division of CPC International Inc.
Borden Kitchens, Borden, Inc.
California Apricot Advisory Board
California Tree Fruit Agreement
Chilean Winter Fruit Association
The Dannon Company, Inc.
Del Monte Corporation
Dole Food Company, Inc.
Kraft General Foods, Inc.

Libby's, Nestlé Food Company
Mott's U.S.A., A division of Cadbury Beverages Inc.
Nabisco Foods Group
Nestlé Chocolate and Confection Company
The Procter & Gamble Company, Inc.
USA Rice Council
Walnut Marketing Board

Index

Almonds
Almond Macaroons, 48
Mini Almond Cheesecakes, 15
Raisin, Oat & Almond Bars, 52
Raspberry Rice aux Amandes, 70
Ambrosia Fruit Custard, 68
Angel Food Cake with Blueberry Yogurt
    Sauce, 16
Apples
Apple Baked Pudding, 83
Apple Bran Loaf, 35
Apple Butter, 88
Apple Chiffon Cake, 19
Apple Cinnamon Dessert, 78
Apple Honeydew Ice, 57
Apple Sauce Bran Muffins, 37
Apple Sauce Glaze, 37
Cinnamon Apple-Nut Muffins, 34
Cranberry Apple Ice, 56
Cranberry Apple Pie with Soft Gingersnap
    Crust, 29
Cranberry-Apple Tart, 24
5-Minute Apple Crisp, 76
Frozen Apple Sauce 'n Fruit Cup, 62
Frozen Yogurt Pie, 26
Golden Apple Cupcakes, 10
Harvest Bundt® Cake, 9
Orange Apple Ice, 56
Apricots
Apricot Crumble, 75
Apricot Frappé, 88
Apricot Mousse, 62
Apricot-Pecan Tassies, 45
Layered Fruit Bars, 44

Baked Truffle Treasures, 43
Bananas
Banana Cookies, 50
Banana-Date Shake, 90
Banana Pineapple Colada, 85
Banana Upside-Down Cake, 14
Cocoa Banana Bars, 48
Cocoa Banana-Nut Bread, 34
Frozen Banana Dessert Cups, 71
Fruited Yogurt Shake, 85
Lemon Banana Yogurt Pops, 64
Sautéed Bananas, 78
Tropical Banana Cake, 13
Bar Cookies
Chocolate Chip Raspberry Jumbles, 46
Cocoa Banana Bars, 48

Cranberry-Orange Muesli Bars, 50
Layered Fruit Bars, 44
Peanut Butter Bars, 51
Raisin, Oat & Almond Bars, 52
Tropical Bar Cookies, 43
Bavarian Rice Cloud with Bittersweet
    Chocolate Sauce, 55
Beverages
Apricot Frappé, 88
Banana-Date Shake, 90
Banana Pineapple Colada, 85
Cranberry Cool, 86
Fruited Yogurt Shake, 85
Iced French Roast, 87
Peach Fizz, 87
Pear Berry Crush, 90
Strawberry Frosty, 88
Bittersweet Chocolate Sauce, 55
Blueberries
Angel Food Cake with Blueberry Yogurt
    Sauce, 16
Blueberry Angel Food Cake Rolls, 8
Blueberry Crisp, 74
Blueberry Orange Loaf, 39
Nutty Blueberry Muffins, 31
Breads (*see also* **Coffeecakes; Muffins**)
Apple Bran Loaf, 35
Blueberry Orange Loaf, 39.
Cocoa Banana-Nut Bread, 34
Lemon Cranberry Loaves, 37
Orange Chocolate Chip Bread, 31
Pineapple-Currant Bread, 32
Brownies
Cocoa Brownies, 41
Painted Desert Brownies, 44

Cakes (*see also* **Cheesecakes**)
Angel Food Cake with Blueberry Yogurt
    Sauce, 16
Apple Chiffon Cake, 19
Banana Upside-Down Cake, 14
Blueberry Angel Food Cake Rolls, 8
Carrot Pudding Cake with Lemon Sauce,
    12
Chocolate Angel Food Cake, 13
Chocolate Orange Delight, 19
Della Robbia Cake, 5
Golden Apple Cupcakes, 10
Harvest Bundt® Cake, 9
Light Mocha Cake with Raspberry Sauce,
    9

Orange Poppy Seed Cake, 16
Peachy Chocolate Cake, 5
Raspberry Shortcake, 14
Tropical Banana Cake, 13
Tropical Fruit Delight, 7
Carrot Pudding Cake with Lemon Sauce, 12
Carrot Raisin Coffee Cake, 38
Cheesecakes
  Chocolate Raspberry Cheesecake, 6
  Creamy Citrus Cheesecake, 18
  Lemony Light Vineyard "Cheesecakes," 6
  Light 'n Luscious Cheesecake, 10
  Mini Almond Cheesecakes, 15
Cherry Yogurt Sesame Pie, 22
Chilled Desserts (*see also* **Parfaits;**
  Puddings & Mousses)
  Chilled Lemonade Dessert, 58
  Cocoa Chiffon Dessert, 64
  Fruit Sparkles, 76
  Jell-O® Sugar Free Jigglers, 59
  Lemon Rice Dessert, 67
  Melon Bubbles, 67
  Nectarine Crème Fraîche, 79
  Tiramisu, 65
Chocolate (*see also* **Brownies**)
  Almond Macaroons, 48
  Baked Truffle Treasures, 43
  Bittersweet Chocolate Sauce, 55
  Chocolate Angel Food Cake, 13
  Chocolate Biscotti, 53
  Chocolate Candy Cookies, 47
  Chocolate Chip Cookies, 41
  Chocolate Chip Raspberry Jumbles, 46
  Chocolate Mousse, 60
  Chocolate Orange Delight, 19
  Chocolate Raspberry Cheesecake, 6
  Cholesterol-Free Chocolate Oatmeal
    Cookies, 51
  Cocoa Banana Bars, 48
  Cocoa Banana-Nut Bread, 34
  Cocoa Chiffon Dessert, 64
  Iced Coffee and Chocolate Pie, 21
  Light Mocha Cake with Raspberry Sauce,
    9
  Lite Chocolate Mint Parfaits, 63
  Mocha-Spice Dessert, 61
  Orange Chocolate Chip Bread, 31
  Peachy Chocolate Cake, 5
  Quick and Creamy Cocoa Dip for Fruit,
    86
  Spectacular Cannolis, 46
  Tiramisu, 65
Cholesterol-Free Chocolate Oatmeal
  Cookies, 51
Cinnamon Apple-Nut Muffins, 34
Cocoa Banana Bars, 48
Cocoa Banana-Nut Bread, 34
Cocoa Brownies, 41

Cocoa Chiffon Dessert, 64
Cocoa Cinnamon Topper, 87
Coffeecakes
  Carrot Raisin Coffee Cake, 38
  Peachy Cinnamon Coffeecake, 33
  Pumpkin-Filled Coffeecake, 35
  Time-Saver Coffeecake, 32
Cookies (*see also* **Bar Cookies; Brownies**)
  Almond Macaroons, 48
  Apricot-Pecan Tassies, 45
  Baked Truffle Treasures, 43
  Banana Cookies, 50
  Chocolate Biscotti, 53
  Chocolate Candy Cookies, 47
  Chocolate Chip Cookies, 41
  Cholesterol-Free Chocolate Oatmeal
    Cookies, 51
  Cranberry Thumbprints, 47
  Jelly-Filled Dainties, 42
  Lemon Cookies, 42
  Mocha Cookies, 47
  Orange Sugar Cookies, 53
  Peanut Butter Cookies, 52
  Spectacular Cannolis, 46
Cottage Cake Muffins, 36
Cranberries
  Cranberry Apple Ice, 56
  Cranberry Apple Pie with Soft Gingersnap
    Crust, 29
  Cranberry-Apple Tart, 24
  Cranberry Cool, 86
  Cranberry Oat Bran Muffins, 33
  Cranberry-Orange Muesli Bars, 50
  Cranberry Sorbet, 57
  Cranberry Thumbprints, 47
  Lemon Cranberry Loaves, 37
Creamy Citrus Cheesecake, 18
Creamy Frozen Yogurt, 71
Crisps & Cobblers
  Apple Cinnamon Dessert, 78
  Apricot Crumble, 75
  Blueberry Crisp, 74
  5-Minute Apple Crisp, 76
Custard Sauce, 82

Deep-Dish Peach Pie, 21
Della Robbia Cake, 5

Easy Pineapple Pie, 24

5-Minute Apple Crisp, 76
Fresh Fruit Parfait, 83
Fresh Fruit Tart, 29
Fresh Peach Sorbet, 67
Frozen Desserts (*see also* **Ices & Sorbets**)
  Creamy Frozen Yogurt, 71
  Frozen Apple Sauce 'n Fruit Cup, 62
  Frozen Banana Dessert Cups, 71

Frozen Desserts (continued)
  Frozen Yogurt Pie, 26
  Grape Yogurt Pops, 68
  Lemon Banana Yogurt Pops, 64
  Peach Ice Cream, 61
  Pumpkin Pie Ice Cream, 58
Fruit Desserts (see also individual fruits)
  Ambrosia Fruit Custard, 68
  Fresh Fruit Parfait, 83
  Fresh Fruit Tart, 29
  Frozen Apple Sauce 'n Fruit Cup, 62
  Fruit Lover's Tart, 22
  Fruit Sparkles, 76
  Fruit Spreads, 90
  Fruit Trifle, 73
  Melon Bubbles, 67
  Melon Cooler Salad, 75
  Meringue Fruit Cups with Custard Sauce,
    82
  Picnic Fruit Tart, 26
  Quick and Creamy Cocoa Dip for Fruit, 86
  Rice Crepes, 80
  Spirited Fruit, 78
  Tropical Fruit Delight, 7
Fruited Yogurt Shake, 85

Golden Apple Cupcakes, 10
Grape Angel Dessert, 80
Grape Yogurt Pops, 68
Grilled Bosc Pears with Walnuts in Apricot
  Yogurt Sauce, 79

Harvest Bundt® Cake, 9

Iced Coffee and Chocolate Pie, 21
Iced French Roast, 87
Ices & Sorbets
  Apple Honeydew Ice, 57
  Cranberry Apple Ice, 56
  Cranberry Sorbet, 57
  Fresh Peach Sorbet, 67
  Nectarine Raspberry Ice, 70
  Orange Apple Ice, 56
  Orange Lemon Sorbet, 68
  Sparkling Lemon Ice, 63
  Strawberry Ice, 61

Jell-O® Sugar Free Jigglers, 59
Jelly-Filled Dainties, 42

Layered Fruit Bars, 44
Lemon
  Carrot Pudding Cake with Lemon Sauce,
    12
  Chilled Lemonade Dessert, 58
  Lemon Banana Yogurt Pops, 64
  Lemon Cookies, 42
  Lemon Ginger Sauce, 85
  Lemon Rice Dessert, 67

  Lemon Sauce, 38
  Lemony Light Vineyard "Cheesecakes," 6
  Light Lemon Meringue Pie, 25
  Lovely Lemon Cheese Pie, 23
  Orange Lemon Sorbet, 68
  Sparkling Lemon Ice, 63
Lemon Cranberry Loaves, 37
Lemon Glazed Peach Muffins, 38
Light 'n Luscious Cheesecake, 10
Light Lemon Meringue Pie, 25
Light Mocha Cake with Raspberry Sauce, 9
Lite Chocolate Mint Parfaits, 63
Lovely Lemon Cheese Pie, 23
Luscious Pumpkin Pie, 28

Melon Bubbles, 67
Melon Cooler Salad, 75
Meringue Fruit Cups with Custard Sauce, 82
Microwave Recipes
  Apple Baked Pudding, 83
  Baked Truffle Treasures, 43
  Blueberry Crisp, 74
  Carrot Pudding Cake with Lemon Sauce,
    12
  Chocolate Raspberry Cheesecake, 6
  Cocoa Banana Bars, 48
  Cocoa Cinnamon Topper, 87
  Fruit Lover's Tart, 22
  Microwave Streusel Pears, 76
  Raisin, Oat & Almond Bars, 52
  Raspberry Rice aux Amandes, 70
Mini Almond Cheesecakes, 15
Mocha
  Iced Coffee and Chocolate Pie, 21
  Iced French Roast, 87
  Light Mocha Cake with Raspberry Sauce,
    9
  Mocha Cookies, 47
  Mocha-Spice Dessert, 61
  Painted Desert Brownies, 44
  Tiramisu, 65
Mousses (see **Puddings & Mousses**)
Muffins
  Apple Sauce Bran Muffins, 37
  Cinnamon Apple-Nut Muffins, 34
  Cottage Cake Muffins, 36
  Cranberry Oat Bran Muffins, 33
  Lemon Glazed Peach Muffins, 38
  Nutty Blueberry Muffins, 31

Nectarine Crème Fraîche, 79
Nectarine Raspberry Ice, 70
Nutty Blueberry Muffins, 31

Orange
  Banana-Date Shake, 90
  Blueberry Orange Loaf, 39
  Chocolate Orange Delight, 19
  Cranberry-Orange Muesli Bars, 50

Orange Apple Ice, 56
Orange Chocolate Chip Bread, 31
Orange Custard Sauce, 80
Orange Lemon Sorbet, 68
Orange Poppy Seed Cake, 16
Orange Sugar Cookies, 53

Painted Desert Brownies, 44
Parfaits
Fresh Fruit Parfait, 83
Lite Chocolate Mint Parfaits, 63
Peach Melba Parfaits, 57
Raspberry Rice aux Amandes, 70
Peaches
Deep-Dish Peach Pie, 21
Della Robbia Cake, 5
Fresh Peach Sorbet, 67
Lemon Glazed Peach Muffins, 38
Mini Almond Cheesecakes, 15
Peach Fizz, 87
Peach Ice Cream, 61
Peach Melba Parfaits, 57
Peachy Chocolate Cake, 5
Peachy Cinnamon Coffeecake, 33
Peanut Butter Bars, 51
Peanut Butter Cookies, 52
Pears
Grilled Bosc Pears with Walnuts in Apricot
    Yogurt Sauce, 79
Microwave Streusel Pears, 76
Pear Berry Crush, 90
Pear Bistro Tart, 28
Picnic Fruit Tart, 26
Pies & Tarts
Cherry Yogurt Sesame Pie, 22
Cranberry Apple Pie with Soft Gingersnap
    Crust, 29
Cranberry-Apple Tart, 24
Deep-Dish Peach Pie, 21
Easy Pineapple Pie, 24
Fresh Fruit Tart, 29
Frozen Yogurt Pie, 26
Fruit Lover's Tart, 22
Iced Coffee and Chocolate Pie, 21
Light Lemon Meringue Pie, 25
Lovely Lemon Cheese Pie, 23
Luscious Pumpkin Pie, 28
Pear Bistro Tart, 28
Picnic Fruit Tart, 26
Pineapple
Banana Pineapple Colada, 85
Easy Pineapple Pie, 24
Pineapple-Currant Bread, 32
Tropical Banana Cake, 13
Tropical Bar Cookies, 43
Puddings & Mousses
Ambrosia Fruit Custard, 68
Apple Baked Pudding, 83
Apricot Mousse, 62

Bavarian Rice Cloud with Bittersweet
    Chocolate Sauce, 55
Chocolate Mousse, 60
Mocha-Spice Dessert, 61
Rice Pudding, 69
Pumpkin
Cottage Cake Muffins, 36
Luscious Pumpkin Pie, 28
Pumpkin-Filled Coffeecake, 35
Pumpkin Pie Ice Cream, 58

Quick and Creamy Cocoa Dip for Fruit, 86
Quick Drizzle Frosting, 36

Raisin, Oat & Almond Bars, 52
Raspberries
Chocolate Chip Raspberry Jumbles, 46
Chocolate Raspberry Cheesecake, 6
Nectarine Raspberry Ice, 70
Peach Melba Parfaits, 57
Pear Berry Crush, 90
Raspberry Rice aux Amandes, 70
Raspberry Sauce, 9, 10
Raspberry Shortcake, 14
Rice Crepes, 80
Rice Pudding, 69

Sauces
Bittersweet Chocolate Sauce, 55
Custard Sauce, 82
Lemon Ginger Sauce, 85
Lemon Sauce, 38
Orange Custard Sauce, 80
Quick and Creamy Cocoa Dip for Fruit, 86
Raspberry Sauce, 9, 10
Sautéed Bananas, 78
Sorbets (*see* **Ices & Sorbets**)
Sparkling Lemon Ice, 63
Spectacular Cannolis, 46
Spirited Fruit, 78
Strawberries
Della Robbia Cake, 5
Strawberries Elegante, 73
Strawberry Frosty, 88
Strawberry Ice, 61
Strawberry Yogurt Angel, 64

Tarts (*see* **Pies & Tarts**)
Time-Saver Coffeecake, 32
Tiramisu, 65
Toppings
Apple Butter, 88
Apple Sauce Glaze, 37
Cocoa Cinnamon Topper, 87
Fruit Spreads, 90
Quick Drizzle Frosting, 36
Tropical Banana Cake, 13
Tropical Bar Cookies, 43
Tropical Fruit Delight, 7

METRIC CONVERSION CHART

VOLUME MEASUREMENT (dry)

⅛ teaspoon = .5 mL
¼ teaspoon = 1 mL
½ teaspoon = 2 mL
¾ teaspoon = 4 mL
1 teaspoon = 5 mL
1 tablespoon = 15 mL
2 tablespoons = 25 mL
¼ cup = 50 mL
⅓ cup = 75 mL
⅔ cup = 150 mL
¾ cup = 175 mL
1 cup = 250 mL
2 cups = 1 pint = 500 mL
3 cups = 750 mL
4 cups = 1 quart = 1 L

DIMENSION

1/16 inch = 2 mm
⅛ inch = 3 mm
¼ inch = 6 mm
½ inch = 1.5 cm
¾ inch = 2 cm
1 inch = 2.5 cm

OVEN TEMPERATURES

250°F = 120°C
275°F = 140°C
300°F = 150°C
325°F = 160°C
350°F = 180°C
375°F = 190°C
400°F = 200°C
425°F = 220°C
450°F = 230°C

VOLUME MEASUREMENT (fluid)

1 fluid ounce (2 tablespoons) = 30 mL
4 fluid ounces (½ cup) = 125 mL
8 fluid ounces (1 cup) = 250 mL
12 fluid ounces (1½ cups) = 375 mL
16 fluid ounces (2 cups) = 500 mL

WEIGHT (MASS)

½ ounce = 15 g
1 ounce = 30 g
3 ounces = 85 g
3.75 ounces = 100 g
4 ounces = 115 g
8 ounces = 225 g
12 ounces = 340 g
16 ounces = 1 pound = 450 g

BAKING PAN SIZES

Utensil	Inches/ Quarts	Metric Volume	Centimeters
Baking or	8×8×2	2 L	20×20 ×5
Cake pan	9×9×2	2.5 L	22×22 ×5
(square or	12×8×2	3 L	30×20 ×5
rectangular)	13×9×2	3.5 L	33×23 ×5
Loaf Pan	8×4×3	1.5 L	20×10 ×7
	9×5×3	2 L	23×13 ×7
Round Layer	8×1½	1.2 L	20×4
Cake Pan	9×1½	1.5 L	23×4
Pie Plate	8×1¼	750 mL	20×3
	9×1¼	1 L	23×3
Baking Dish	1 quart	1 L	
or	1½ quart	1.5 L	
Casserole	2 quart	2 L	